3745

WITHDRAWN

At Issue

What Are the Jobs of the Future?

Other Books in the At Issue Series:

At Issue

What Are the Jobs of the Future?

Roman Espejo, Book Editor

GREENHAVEN PRESS
A part of Gale, Cengage Learning

GALE
CENGAGE Learning·

Farmington Hills, Mich • San Francisco • New York • Waterville, Maine
Meriden, Conn • Mason, Ohio • Chicago

Patricia Coryell, *Vice President & Publisher, New Products & GVRL*
Douglas Dentino, *Manager, New Products*
Judy Galens, *Acquisitions Editor*

For more information, contact:
Greenhaven Press
27500 Drake Rd.
Farmington Hills, MI 48331-3535
Or you can visit our Internet site at gale.cengage.com

Articles in Greenhaven Press anthologies are often edited for length to meet page requirements. In addition, original titles of these works are changed to clearly present the main thesis and to explicitly indicate the author's opinion. Every effort is made to ensure that Greenhaven Press accurately reflects the original intent of the authors. Every effort has been made to trace the owners of copyrighted material.

Cover photograph copyright © Images.com/Corbis.

LIBRARY OF CONGRESS CATALOGING-IN-PUBLICATION DATA

What are the jobs of the future? / Roman Espejo, book editor.
    pages cm. -- (At issue)
    Includes bibliographical references and index.
    ISBN 978-0-7377-7199-2 (hardcover) -- ISBN 978-0-7377-7200-5 (pbk.)
    1. Vocational guidance. 2. Occupations--Forecasting. I. Espejo, Roman, 1977-
    HF5381.W472 2015
    331.702--dc23
                                                                  2014041142

Printed in Mexico
1 2 3 4 5 6 7 19 18 17 16 15

Contents

Introduction

Lyft is for getting a ride. Airbnb is for booking a room. TaskRabbit is for finding someone to run an errand. What do they have in common? They are a few of the tech startups shaping the so-called sharing economy. Also known as the peer-to-peer economy and collaborative consumption, it's the burgeoning online and mobile marketplace of hiring or renting directly between individuals. "You might think this is no different from running a bed-and-breakfast, owning a time-share or participating in a car pool. But technology has reduced transaction costs, making sharing assets cheaper and easier than ever—and therefore possible on a much larger scale,"[1] insists *The Economist* in a March 2013 article. "The big change is the availability of more data about people and things, which allows physical assets to be disaggregated and consumed as services."

Another big change is how the sharing economy is impacting how people make a living. Lyft drivers use their own cars to shuttle people around, earning an attractive $35 an hour, according to the company's website. Airbnb hosts rent out their spare rooms or property, generating significant income in high-priced areas. In a 2012 study by Airbnb, 56 percent of its hosts in San Francisco reported that rental money went to their mortgage or rent, and 46 percent said they spent it on everyday living expenses. And "TaskRabbits" offer their time or skills for hire to perform small jobs; for some, it's become a full-time occupation. "For two years, this has been my main source of income—just riding my bikes

---

1. *Economist*, "Peer-to-Peer Rental: The Rise of the Sharing Economy," March 9, 2013. http://www.economist.com/news/leaders/21573104-internet-everything-hire-rise -sharing-economy.

around, seeing the sights, picking up random stuff,"[2] Justin Prim, a bike messenger, tells ABC's *Nightline.*

In fact, the sharing economy is seen as spurring job creation while the nation recovers from last decade's recession. Although the United States as a whole recovered most of these lost jobs by mid-2014, two-thirds of states have not. "The sharing economy offers enormous potential to create jobs. Sharing leverages a wide variety of resources and lowers barriers to starting small businesses,"[3] declare the nonprofit news portal Shareable and the Sustainable Economies Law Center in their 2013 report, *Policies for Shareable Cities: A Policy Primer for Urban Leaders.* The report contends that the economic benefits are maintained at the local level, keeping profits and employment away from the monopoly of corporations. "Sharing is also at the heart of the employment model that is designed to keep wealth and jobs in the community: cooperatives. In the age of global economics, where even money spent locally can quickly slip from local communities, fostering cooperative enterprise creates local jobs that are rooted securely in the community,"[4] the report states.

Furthermore, some commentators suggest that jobs in the sharing economy offer the flexibility and autonomy a conventional career does not, making it preferable to many workers. "Clearly we're increasingly piecing together livings through mixes of Gigs—part-time, freelance, starting our own businesses, etc.,"[5] asserts Micha Kaufman, chief executive officer and cofounder of Fiverr, an online marketplace for services. "Traditionally, there was one, rigid way to make it: climb the

2. Quoted in Rebecca Jarvis, Ben Newman, and Lauren Effron, "Outsourcing Your Errands: TaskRabbit Allows People to Rent Themselves Out for Odd Jobs," *Nightline,* June 20, 2014. http://abcnews.go.com/Business/outsourcing-errands-taskrabbit -people-rent-odd-jobs/story?id=24231980.
3. SELC, "Seven Job Creation Strategies for Shareable Cities," Shareable, December 23, 2013. http://www.shareable.net/blog/seven-job-creation-strategies-for-shareable-cities.
4. Ibid.
5. Micha Kaufman, "Trust Each Other, the Sharing Economy Is Here to Stay," *Forbes,* May 16, 2014. http://www.forbes.com/sites/michakaufman/2014/05/16/sharing economy.

ladder and rise to the top of your company. But that doesn't make sense in a Gig-based type of world," Kaufman adds. "Instead, as certain people enter the sharing economy out of need, what they discover is that it affords them a freedom they can't find in a traditional setting, from doing what they love to scheduling their various Gigs in such a way that they have time between projects to get healthy, go on vacation, and be with their loved ones."[6]

Nonetheless, the sharing economy has its share of critics. For instance, the current lack of regulations governing such services as Lyft and Airbnb has caused an uproar among taxi companies and hotel owners. "That's why I'm afraid the much-celebrated 'sharing economy'—the catch-all name for 'peer-to-peer' firms that connect people for the purposes of distributing, sharing, and reusing goods and services—is likely to produce more fights than profits. States could be embroiled for years in political, legal, commercial and environmental battles related to sharing,"[7] writes Joe Mathews, California senior research fellow at the New America Foundation, in a *Time* editorial. Mathews believes that the business model is a Pandora's Box of risks, liabilities, and complications. "So my bid to watch your dog while you're on vacation—and yours to drive me to the airport—is at once freeing and full of dangers. Who's responsible if your dog bites my kid while in my care? What kind of car insurance, training and licensing do you need to shuttle me safely? What, if anything, do we owe to the kennel workers and cabbies who lose work? And who decides how we govern all of this?," he speculates.

Additionally, it is argued that participating in the sharing economy is not as appealing as it seems, since its popularity reflects, not prosperity and freedom, but hardship and desperation among its out-of-work members trying to make a

---

6. Ibid.
7. Joe Mathews, "The Sharing Economy Boom Is About to Bust," *Time*, June 27, 2014. http://time.com/2924778/airbnb-uber-sharing-economy.

living. "At the risk of bragging, my immigrant parents were clearly trendsetters in this area. They typically rented or borrowed spare rooms (rather than stay at motels/hotels, or in a regular apartment), cars, clothing, shoes or pretty much anything they couldn't afford to own themselves—which was just about everything,"[8] claims Steven Strauss, an adjunct lecturer in public policy at Harvard Kennedy School. "The 21st century sharing economy isn't being embraced because people want 'lightweight (asset-free) living.' It's usually embraced for the same reasons it was embraced in the 1920s–1930s. For many people, there's not any other choice." Furthermore, Strauss adds that full-timers in the sharing economy will not have "a regular salary, paid vacations, employer-provided health insurance, or a chance of getting rich from an IPO [initial public offering]."

The sharing economy is closely tied to technological advances, particularly innovations in Internet technology, developments in mobile communications, and breakthroughs in software and electronics. *At Issue: What Are the Jobs of the Future?* examines these impacts on how people work, how work is changing, and more. The range of commentaries, analyses, and forecasts selected for this volume represent the issues facing modern workers and businesses on the cusp of transformation.

8. Steven Strauss, "'Welcome' to the Sharing Economy—Also Known as the Collapse of the American Dream," *Huffington Post*, December 29, 2013. http://www .huffingtonpost.com/steven-strauss/welcome-to-the-sharing-economy_b_4516707 .html.

1

Many Jobs Will Be Replaced by Technological Innovation

Bernard Condon and Paul Wiseman

Bernard Condon and Paul Wiseman are both business writers for the Associated Press.

Obliterated by technological innovation, mid-pay, mid-skilled jobs lost during the Great Recession of 2007–2009 are not coming back. Transforming economies worldwide, automation, devices, software, and apps are eliminating entire fields of employment. Jobs involving repetitive tasks are the most vulnerable, but eventually task-juggling managers and supervisors will be victims of innovation. Moreover, employers that relied on cheaper, more efficient technology during the recession have not rehired workers, and startups and new businesses now hire fewer staff. Unlike earlier innovations that created more jobs, technology will threaten to replace workers in highly skilled occupations. Even the most optimistic economists have some doubt that the gains will outweigh the losses.

Five years after the start of the Great Recession [in 2007], the toll is terrifyingly clear: Millions of middle-class jobs have been lost in developed countries the world over.

And the situation is even worse than it appears.

Most of the jobs will never return, and millions more are likely to vanish as well, say experts who study the labor market. What's more, these jobs aren't just being lost to China and other developing countries, and they aren't just factory work. Increasingly, jobs are disappearing in the service sector, home to two-thirds of all workers.

They're being obliterated by technology.

Year after year, the software that runs computers and an array of other machines and devices becomes more sophisticated and powerful and capable of doing more efficiently tasks that humans have always done. For decades, science fiction warned of a future when we would be architects of our own obsolescence, replaced by our machines; an Associated Press [AP] analysis finds that the future has arrived.

The Global Economy Is Being Reshaped

"The jobs that are going away aren't coming back," says Andrew McAfee, principal research scientist at the Center for Digital Business at the Massachusetts Institute of Technology and co-author of "Race Against the Machine." "I have never seen a period where computers demonstrated as many skills and abilities as they have over the past seven years."

In the United States, half the 7.5 million jobs lost during the Great Recession were in industries that pay middle-class wages.

The global economy is being reshaped by machines that generate and analyze vast amounts of data; by devices such as smartphones and tablet computers that let people work just about anywhere, even when they're on the move; by smarter, nimbler robots; and by services that let businesses rent computing power when they need it, instead of installing expensive equipment and hiring IT [information technology] staffs to run it. Whole employment categories, from secretaries to travel agents, are starting to disappear.

"There's no sector of the economy that's going to get a pass," says Martin Ford, who runs a software company and wrote "The Lights in the Tunnel," a book predicting widespread job losses. "It's everywhere."

The numbers startle even labor economists. In the United States, half the 7.5 million jobs lost during the Great Recession were in industries that pay middle-class wages, ranging from $38,000 to $68,000. But only 2 percent of the 3.5 million jobs gained since the recession ended in June 2009 are in midpay industries. Nearly 70 percent are in low-pay industries, 29 percent in industries that pay well.

In the 17 European countries that use the euro as their currency, the numbers are even worse. Almost 4.3 million low-pay jobs have been gained since mid-2009, but the loss of midpay jobs has never stopped. A total of 7.6 million disappeared from January 2008 through last June.

Experts warn that this "hollowing out" of the middle-class workforce is far from over. They predict the loss of millions more jobs as technology becomes even more sophisticated and reaches deeper into our lives. Maarten Goos, an economist at the University of Leuven in Belgium, says Europe could double its middle-class job losses.

Some occupations are beneficiaries of the march of technology, such as software engineers and app designers for smartphones and tablet computers. Overall, though, technology is eliminating far more jobs than it is creating.

To understand the impact technology is having on middle-class jobs in developed countries, the AP analyzed employment data from 20 countries; tracked changes in hiring by industry, pay and task; compared job losses and gains during recessions and expansions over the past four decades; and interviewed economists, technology experts, robot manufacturers, software developers, entrepreneurs and people in the labor force who ranged from CEOs to the unemployed.

The AP's Key Findings

- For more than three decades, technology has reduced the number of jobs in manufacturing. Robots and other machines controlled by computer programs work faster and make fewer mistakes than humans. Now, that same efficiency is being unleashed in the service economy, which employs more than two-thirds of the workforce in developed countries. Technology is eliminating jobs in office buildings, retail establishments and other businesses consumers deal with every day.

- Technology is being adopted by every kind of organization that employs people. It's replacing workers in large corporations and small businesses, established companies and start-ups. It's being used by schools, colleges and universities; hospitals and other medical facilities; nonprofit organizations and the military.

- The most vulnerable workers are doing repetitive tasks that programmers can write software for—an accountant checking a list of numbers, an office manager filing forms, a paralegal reviewing documents for key words to help in a case. As software becomes even more sophisticated, victims are expected to include those who juggle tasks, such as supervisors and managers—workers who thought they were protected by a college degree.

- Thanks to technology, companies in the Standard & Poor's 500 stock index reported one-third more profit the past year than they earned the year before the Great Recession. They've also expanded their businesses, but total employment, at 21.1 million, has declined by a half-million.

- Start-ups account for much of the job growth in developed economies, but software is allowing entrepreneurs to launch businesses with a third fewer employees than in the 1990s. There is less need for administrative support and back-office jobs that handle accounting, payroll and benefits.

- It's becoming a self-serve world. Instead of relying on someone else in the workplace or our personal lives, we use technology to do tasks ourselves. Some find this frustrating; others like the feeling of control. Either way, this trend will only grow as software permeates our lives.

- Technology is replacing workers in developed countries regardless of their politics, policies and laws. Union rules and labor laws may slow the dismissal of employees, but no country is attempting to prohibit organizations from using technology that allows them to operate more efficiently—and with fewer employees.

The developed world may face years of high middle-class unemployment, social discord, divisive politics, falling living standards and dashed hopes.

Some analysts reject the idea that technology has been a big job killer. They note that the collapse of the housing market in the U.S., Ireland, Spain and other countries and the ensuing global recession wiped out millions of middle-class construction and factory jobs. In their view, governments could bring many of the jobs back if they would put aside worries about their heavy debts and spend more. Others note that jobs continue to be lost to China, India and other countries in the developing world.

But to the extent technology has played a role, it raises the specter of high unemployment even after economic growth accelerates. Some economists say millions of middle-class workers must be retrained to do other jobs if they hope to get work again. Others are more hopeful. They note that technological change over the centuries eventually has created more jobs than it destroyed, though the wait can be long and painful.

A common refrain: The developed world may face years of high middle-class unemployment, social discord, divisive politics, falling living standards and dashed hopes.

Truly a Jobless Recovery

In the U.S., the economic recovery that started in June 2009 has been called the third straight "jobless recovery."

But that's a misnomer. The jobs came back after the first two.

Most recessions since World War II were followed by a surge in new jobs as consumers started spending again and companies hired to meet the new demand. In the months after recessions ended in 1991 and 2001, there was no familiar snap-back, but all the jobs had returned in less than three years.

But 42 months after the Great Recession ended, the U.S. has gained only 3.5 million, or 47 percent, of the 7.5 million jobs that were lost. The 17 countries that use the euro had 3.5 million fewer jobs last June than in December 2007.

This has truly been a jobless recovery, and the lack of midpay jobs is almost entirely to blame.

Fifty percent of the U.S. jobs lost were in midpay industries, but Moody's Analytics, a research firm, says just 2 percent of the 3.5 million jobs gained are in that category. After the four previous recessions, at least 30 percent of jobs created—and as many as 46 percent—were in midpay industries.

Other studies that group jobs differently show a similar drop in middle-class work.

Some of the most startling studies have focused on mid-skill, midpay jobs that require tasks that follow well-defined procedures and are repeated throughout the day. Think travel agents, salespeople in stores, office assistants and back-office workers like benefits managers and payroll clerks, as well as machine operators and other factory jobs. An August 2012 paper by economists Henry Siu of the University of British Columbia and Nir Jaimovich of Duke University found these kinds of jobs comprise fewer than half of all jobs, yet accounted for nine of 10 of all losses in the Great Recession. And they have kept disappearing in the economic recovery.

Companies in the recession learned to be more efficient, and they're not going to go back.

Webb Wheel Products makes parts for truck brakes, which involves plenty of repetitive work. Its newest employee is the Doosan V550M, and it's a marvel. It can spin a 130-pound brake drum like a child's top, smooth its metal surface, then drill holes—all without missing a beat. And it doesn't take vacations or "complain about anything," says Dwayne Ricketts, president of the Cullman, Ala., company.

Thanks to computerized machines, Webb Wheel hasn't added a factory worker in three years, though it's making 300,000 more drums annually, a 25 percent increase.

"Everyone is waiting for the unemployment rate to drop, but I don't know if it will much," Ricketts says. "Companies in the recession learned to be more efficient, and they're not going to go back."

In Europe, companies couldn't go back even if they wanted to. The 17 countries that use the euro slipped into another recession 14 months ago, in November 2011. The current unemployment rate is a record 11.8 percent.

European companies had been using technology to replace midpay workers for years, and now that has accelerated.

"The recessions have amplified the trend," says Goos, the Belgian economist. "New jobs are being created, but not the middle-pay ones."

In Canada, a 2011 study by economists at the University of British Columbia and York University in Toronto found a similar pattern of middle-class losses, though they were working with older data. In the 15 years through 2006, the share of total jobs held by many midpay, midskill occupations shrank. The share held by foremen fell 37 percent, workers in administrative and senior clerical roles fell 18 percent and those in sales and service fell 12 percent.

In Japan, a 2009 report from Hitotsubashi University in Tokyo documented a "substantial" drop in midpay, midskill jobs in the five years through 2005, and linked it to technology.

Developing economies have been spared the technological onslaught—for now. Countries like Brazil and China are still growing middle-class jobs because they're shifting from export-driven to consumer-based economies. But even they are beginning to use more machines in manufacturing. The cheap labor they relied on to make goods from apparel to electronics is no longer so cheap as their living standards rise.

One example is Sunbird Engineering, a Hong Kong firm that makes mirror frames for heavy trucks at a factory in southern China. Salaries at its plant in Dongguan have nearly tripled from $80 a month in 2005 to $225 today. "Automation is the obvious next step," CEO Bill Pike says.

Sunbird is installing robotic arms that drill screws into a mirror assembly, work now done by hand. The machinery will allow the company to eliminate two positions on a 13-person assembly line. Pike hopes that additional automation will allow the company to reduce another five or six jobs from the line.

"By automating, we can outlive the labor cost increases inevitable in China," Pike says. "Those who automate in China will win the battle of increased costs."

Most jobs cut in the U.S. and Europe weren't moved. No one got them. They vanished.

Foxconn Technology Group, which assembles iPhones at factories in China, unveiled plans in 2011 to install one million robots over three years.

A recent headline in the China Daily newspaper: "Chinese robot wars set to erupt."

The Villian of the Story

Candidates for U.S. president last year never tired of telling Americans how jobs were being shipped overseas. China, with its vast army of cheaper labor and low-value currency, was easy to blame.

But most jobs cut in the U.S. and Europe weren't moved. No one got them. They vanished. And the villain in this story—a clever software engineer working in Silicon Valley or the high-tech hub around Heidelberg, Germany—isn't so easy to hate.

"It doesn't have political appeal to say the reason we have a problem is we're so successful in technology," says Joseph Stiglitz, a Nobel Prize-winning economist at Columbia University. "There's no enemy there."

Unless you count family and friends and the person staring at you in the mirror. The uncomfortable truth is technology is killing jobs with the help of ordinary consumers by enabling them to quickly do tasks that workers used to do full time, for salaries.

Use a self-checkout lane at the supermarket or drugstore? A worker behind a cash register used to do that.

Buy clothes without visiting a store? You've taken work from a salesman.

Click "accept" in an email invitation to attend a meeting? You've pushed an office assistant closer to unemployment.

Book your vacation using an online program? You've helped lay off a travel agent. Perhaps at American Express Co., which announced this month that it plans to cut 5,400 jobs, mainly in its travel business, as more of its customers shift to online portals to plan trips.

Software is picking out worrisome blots in medical scans, running trains without conductors, driving cars without drivers, spotting profits in stocks trades in milliseconds, analyzing Twitter traffic to tell where to sell certain snacks, sifting through documents for evidence in court cases, recording power usage beamed from digital utility meters at millions of homes, and sorting returned library books.

Technology gives rise to "cheaper products and cool services," says David Autor, an economist at MIT, one of the first to document tech's role in cutting jobs. "But if you lose your job, that is slim compensation."

Even the most commonplace technologies—take, say, email—are making it tough for workers to get jobs, including ones with MBAs [Master of Business Administration], like Roshanne Redmond, a former project manager at a commercial real estate developer.

These are jobs that used to fill cubicles at almost every company—clerks paying bills and ordering supplies, benefits managers filing health-care forms and IT experts helping with computer crashes.

"I used to get on the phone, talk to a secretary and coordinate calendars," Redmond says. "Now, things are done by computer."

Technology is used by companies to run leaner and smarter in good times and bad, but never more than in bad. In a recession, sales fall and companies cut jobs to save money. Then they turn to technology to do tasks people used to do. And that's when it hits them: They realize they don't have to re-hire the humans when business improves, or at least not as many.

The Hackett Group, a consultant on back-office jobs, estimates 2 million of them in finance, human resources, information technology and procurement have disappeared in the U.S. and Europe since the Great Recession. It pins the blame for more than half of the losses on technology. These are jobs that used to fill cubicles at almost every company—clerks paying bills and ordering supplies, benefits managers filing health-care forms and IT experts helping with computer crashes.

"The effect of (technology) on white-collar jobs is huge, but it's not obvious," says MIT's McAfee. Companies "don't put out a press release saying we're not hiring again because of machines."

No End to Computers in the Workplace

What hope is there for the future?

Historically, new companies and new industries have been the incubator of new jobs. Start-up companies no more than five years old are big sources of new jobs in developed economies. In the U.S., they accounted for 99 percent of new private sector jobs in 2005, according to a study by the University of Maryland's John Haltiwanger and two other economists.

But even these companies are hiring fewer people. The average new business employed 4.7 workers when it opened its doors in 2011, down from 7.6 in the 1990s, according to a Labor Department study released last March.

Technology is probably to blame, wrote the report's authors, Eleanor Choi and James Spletzer. Entrepreneurs no longer need people to do clerical and administrative tasks to help them get their businesses off the ground.

In the old days—say, 10 years ago—"you'd need an assistant pretty early to coordinate everything—or you'd pay a huge opportunity cost for the entrepreneur or the president to set up a meeting," says Jeff Connally, CEO [chief executive officer] of CMIT Solutions, a technology consultancy to small businesses.

Now technology means "you can look at your calendar and everybody else's calendar and—bing!—you've set up a meeting." So no assistant gets hired.

Eventually . . . software will threaten the livelihoods of doctors, lawyers and other highly skilled professionals.

Entrepreneur Andrew Schrage started the financial advice website Money Crashers in 2009 with a partner and one freelance writer. The bare-bones start-up was only possible, Schrage says, because of technology that allowed the company to get online help with accounting and payroll and other support functions without hiring staff.

"Had I not had access to cloud computing and outsourcing, I estimate that I would have needed 5-10 employees to begin this venture," Schrage says. "I doubt I would have been able to launch my business."

Technological innovations have been throwing people out of jobs for centuries. But they eventually created more work, and greater wealth, than they destroyed. Ford, the author and software engineer, thinks there is reason to believe that this time will be different. He sees virtually no end to the inroads of computers into the workplace. Eventually, he says, software will threaten the livelihoods of doctors, lawyers and other highly skilled professionals.

Many economists are encouraged by history and think the gains eventually will outweigh the losses. But even they have doubts.

"What's different this time is that digital technologies show up in every corner of the economy," says McAfee, a self-described "digital optimist." "Your tablet (computer) is just two or three years old, and it's already taken over our lives."

Peter Lindert, an economist at the University of California, Davis, says the computer is more destructive than innovations in the Industrial Revolution because the pace at which it is upending industries makes it hard for people to adapt.

Occupations that provided middle-class lifestyles for generations can disappear in a few years. Utility meter readers are just one example. As power companies began installing so-called smart readers outside homes, the number of meter readers in the U.S. plunged from 56,000 in 2001 to 36,000 in 2010, according to the Labor Department.

In 10 years? That number is expected to be zero.

2

Coming to an Office Near You

The Economist

The Economist is a weekly British-based publication focusing on international politics and business news.

From the Industrial Revolution to the ongoing digital revolution, technological innovation has always eliminated jobs. But while it has destroyed some jobs and even industries, it has always created new and better jobs, meaning that workers are not relegated to unemployment. However, the pitfalls of technological disruption arrive faster than the benefits for workers, and capitalists and the highest-skilled employees initially gain the most wealth. Governments must ensure that policies assist the dislocation of the most vulnerable workers as wages stall and income gaps widen. Improving education should foster skills that cannot be replaced by computers, such as creativity and cognitive abilities. Public money—not minimum wage increases—should also be provided to workers to maintain reasonable incomes.

Innovation, the elixir of progress, has always cost people their jobs. In the Industrial Revolution artisan weavers were swept aside by the mechanical loom. Over the past 30 years the digital revolution has displaced many of the mid-skill jobs that underpinned 20th-century middle-class life. Typists, ticket agents, bank tellers and many production-line jobs have been dispensed with, just as the weavers were.

For those, including this newspaper, who believe that technological progress has made the world a better place, such churn is a natural part of rising prosperity. Although innovation kills some jobs, it creates new and better ones, as a more productive society becomes richer and its wealthier inhabitants demand more goods and services. A hundred years ago one in three American workers was employed on a farm. Today less than 2% of them produce far more food. The millions freed from the land were not consigned to joblessness, but found better-paid work as the economy grew more sophisticated. Today the pool of secretaries has shrunk, but there are ever more computer programmers and web designers.

Remember Ironbridge

Optimism remains the right starting-point, but for workers the dislocating effects of technology may make themselves evident faster than its benefits. Even if new jobs and wonderful products emerge, in the short term income gaps will widen, causing huge social dislocation and perhaps even changing politics. Technology's impact will feel like a tornado, hitting the rich world first, but eventually sweeping through poorer countries too. No government is prepared for it.

Computers are increasingly able to perform complicated tasks more cheaply and effectively than people.

Why be worried? It is partly just a matter of history repeating itself. In the early part of the Industrial Revolution the rewards of increasing productivity went disproportionately to capital; later on, labour reaped most of the benefits. The pattern today is similar. The prosperity unleashed by the digital revolution has gone overwhelmingly to the owners of capital and the highest-skilled workers. Over the past three decades, labour's share of output has shrunk globally from 64% to 59%. Meanwhile, the share of income going to the top 1% in America has risen from around 9% in the 1970s to 22% today. Unemployment is at alarming levels in much of the rich

25

world, and not just for cyclical reasons. In 2000, 65% of working-age Americans were in work; since then the proportion has fallen, during good years as well as bad, to the current level of 59%.

Worse, it seems likely that this wave of technological disruption to the job market has only just started. From driverless cars to clever household gadgets, innovations that already exist could destroy swathes of jobs that have hitherto been untouched. The public sector is one obvious target: it has proved singularly resistant to tech-driven reinvention. But the steep change in what computers can do will have a powerful effect on middle-class jobs in the private sector too.

Until now the jobs most vulnerable to machines were those that involved routine, repetitive tasks. But thanks to the exponential rise in processing power and the ubiquity of digitised information ("big data"), computers are increasingly able to perform complicated tasks more cheaply and effectively than people. Clever industrial robots can quickly "learn" a set of human actions. Services may be even more vulnerable. Computers can already detect intruders in a closed-circuit camera picture more reliably than a human can. By comparing reams of financial or biometric data, they can often diagnose fraud or illness more accurately than any number of accountants or doctors. One recent study by academics at Oxford University suggests that 47% of today's jobs could be automated in the next two decades.

At the same time, the digital revolution is transforming the process of innovation itself, as our special report explains. Thanks to off-the-shelf code from the internet and platforms that host services (such as Amazon's cloud computing), provide distribution (Apple's app store) and offer marketing (Facebook), the number of digital startups has exploded. Just as computer-games designers invented a product that humanity never knew it needed but now cannot do without, so these firms will no doubt dream up new goods and services to employ millions. But for now they are singularly light on workers. When Instagram, a popular photo-sharing site, was sold to Facebook for about $1 billion in 2012, it had 30m [million] customers and employed 13 people. Kodak, which filed for bankruptcy a few months earlier, employed 145,000 people in its heyday.

The problem is one of timing as much as anything. Google now employs 46,000 people. But it takes years for new industries to grow, whereas the disruption a startup causes to incumbents is felt sooner. Airbnb may turn homeowners with spare rooms into entrepreneurs, but it poses a direct threat to the lower end of the hotel business—a massive employer.

The main way in which governments can help their people through this dislocation is through education systems.

No Time to Be Timid

If this analysis is halfway correct, the social effects will be huge. Many of the jobs most at risk are lower down the ladder (logistics, haulage), whereas the skills that are least vulnerable to automation (creativity, managerial expertise) tend to be higher up, so median wages are likely to remain stagnant for some time and income gaps are likely to widen.

Anger about rising inequality is bound to grow, but politicians will find it hard to address the problem. Shunning progress would be as futile now as the Luddites' protests against mechanised looms were in the 1810s, because any country that tried to stop would be left behind by competitors eager to embrace new technology. The freedom to raise taxes on the rich to punitive levels will be similarly constrained by the mobility of capital and highly skilled labour.

The main way in which governments can help their people through this dislocation is through education systems. One of the reasons for the improvement in workers' fortunes in the latter part of the Industrial Revolution was because schools were built to educate them—a dramatic change at the time. Now those schools themselves need to be changed, to foster the creativity that humans will need to set them apart from computers. There should be less rote-learning and more critical thinking. Technology itself will help, whether through MOOCs (massive open online courses) or even video games that simulate the skills needed for work.

The definition of "a state education" may also change. Far more money should be spent on preschooling, since the cognitive abilities and social skills that children learn in their first few years define much of their future potential. And adults will need continuous education. State education may well involve a year of study to be taken later in life, perhaps in stages.

Yet however well people are taught, their abilities will remain unequal, and in a world which is increasingly polarised economically, many will find their job prospects dimmed and wages squeezed. The best way of helping them is not, as many on the left seem to think, to push up minimum wages. Jacking up the floor too far would accelerate the shift from human workers to computers. Better to top up low wages with public money so that anyone who works has a reasonable income, through a bold expansion of the tax credits that countries such as America and Britain use.

Innovation has brought great benefits to humanity. Nobody in their right mind would want to return to the world of handloom weavers. But the benefits of technological progress are unevenly distributed, especially in the early stages of each new wave, and it is up to governments to spread them. In the 19th century it took the threat of revolution to bring about progressive reforms. Today's governments would do well to start making the changes needed before their people get angry.

3

Data Scientist Is the Most Promising Job of the Future

Hilary Mason, interviewed by Greg A. Smith for Credit Suisse.

Hilary Mason is the chief scientist at Bitly, a web-based curation service that supports the social networking activities of businesses, nonprofits, and government agencies. Greg A. Smith is a finance professional who conducted the interview for the international banking firm Credit Suisse.

Called the "sexiest job of the twenty-first century," the data scientist will be in high demand as businesses and other organizations seek to better leverage the growing universe of information they possess. A new profession, the data scientist not only understands business problems but has the technical abilities to extract, analyze, and process information, and to pose the right questions and translate the findings for others. With master's programs recently launched in the field, data scientists currently come from diverse scientific and academic backgrounds; however, finding job candidates with useful experience is difficult.

Hilary Mason is the chief scientist at Bitly, a web-based "curation" tool that allows users to save, share, and discover new things on the web. To do so, Bitly tracks social media data with the focus and intensity of a scientist trying to unravel the human genome. In other words, they're data scientists. But Hilary Mason, Bitly's chief scientist, calls them "awesome nerds"—tech-savvy science types who not only know how to mine the gold from an endlessly expanding information universe, but also know how to talk to normal humans about what they've discovered. Credit Suisse sat down with Mason to find out who these people are and what they actually do.

The Sexiest Job of the 21st Century

Credit Suisse: The Harvard Business Review called data scientist the sexiest job of the 21st century. You call them awesome nerds. So what exactly is it that they do?

Hilary Mason: A data scientist is somebody who can understand business problems, who can actually do an analysis that informs a solution to a problem and then communicate it successfully. But they do it by using a skill set that has never before been combined into one profession.

The basic skills are the technical abilities to get data out of a system and process it, and perhaps build infrastructure on top of it—that's engineering and hacking. Then you need to do an analysis—that's statistics, linear algebra and probability theory on the math side. And then the last piece is the combination of social science and curiosity and understanding business—asking the right questions, translating them into your mathematical and engineering analysis, then translating that into something you can actually talk to other human beings about.

A lot of the companies hiring data scientists are hiring their first one, and that means they don't have an infrastructure for mentoring or cultivating them internally.

Where do you find these people? Are universities teaching data science?

I haven't hired anyone with a data science master's degree because the programs are just starting. Data scientists come from all different fields, including a lot of academic scientists who are leaving academia and who can be trained to communicate. I'm a computer scientist, and I work with an astrophysicist, a physicist, another computer scientist and a mathematician. But I have peers in other companies and universities who come to it from political science and psychology. It's such a young field that people are arriving in it from many different directions.

An Elite Position in Demand

It has fast become an elite position in a healthy IT [information technology] job market. There are nearly 5 million IT jobs in the U.S. alone. Is supply meeting demand?

It's very hard to find people who have any useful experience. A lot of the companies hiring data scientists are hiring their first one, and that means they don't have an infrastructure for mentoring or cultivating them internally. And people with even a little bit of experience are very hard to come by.

But I've read about data neophytes taking a course or two, then going on to solve complex problems posted online. Some might say data science may be easier than you'd think.

I am a little skeptical of that. Large companies can package algorithmic problems they need to solve and put a challenge online. But that's a very defined error metric you're trying to optimize. It's like that little wrench you get from IKEA in your toolbox. When you need it, it is the perfect tool. But most of the time it's not the best tool for solving your data problem. The job of the data scientist is to know what the problem is in the first place.

So who needs a data scientist?

You need a data scientist when you think you could be making better decisions than you are based on available data. Take what we do at Bitly. In the past, a marketer would just look at their own data and work with their own materials. But now we know what everyone on the Internet is paying attention to, and you can use that to inform your practice. And you can build products that just weren't possible before. The way I usually describe the whole thing is: Level 1 is using data to make better decisions about the business you have now. Level 2 is taking your business in a direction that was never possible without the data.

The Person with the Data

Where does the data chief sit on the company totem pole?

My friend D.J. Patil, who actually co-wrote the Harvard article you referred to at the beginning, has the best way of describing this: You should think about your chief data scientist as your "Spock on the bridge." He's not going to be issuing the orders, but when Captain Kirk has to make a decision, that's the person he will turn to.

You really want somebody who can internalize your data and systems, and just knows how to answer a question.

How do you structure a data team?

You have a bunch of pieces—the data warehouse, the analysis infrastructure and the interface with other groups that need to use the data. So data teams tend to do a number of different things. They do business analytics: How healthy is my business? If I do X, do I make more money? They do product development: What is this cohort of users who came into my product at this time doing in the product, and what does that mean for the design? They build things like recommendation algorithms, search engines and spam filters. And they do a lot of research.

Why can't you just bring someone in when you need them?

Hiring contractors can work, but you really want somebody who can internalize your data and systems, and just knows how to answer a question.

You keep coming back to that—knowing the right questions.

It's not the kind of question as much as how you ask it. And that really goes back to following the scientific method: have a theory, look at the data and see if it confirms your theory, and then make a decision. So I can show you a graph, but we might have very different stories that describe what we're seeing in that graph. And we might not be able to agree on an interpretation unless we've agreed on what we're studying in the first place.

How do you convince your CEO [chief executive officer] to go along with your proposed solutions to business problems?

It's very hard to argue with the person with the data.

4

Software Engineer Is a Promising Job of the Future

John R. Platt

John R. Platt is a writer who frequently contributes to Today's Engineer, Scientific American, *and* Mother Nature Network.

Jobs in software engineering are some of the fastest growing, with software embedded in nearly all devices and products. Software engineers are valuable because of the low success rate of software projects; engineers operating by standard development principles are sought to prevent costly delays and failures. Additionally, the number of employed software engineers has increased 25 percent over the past decade, and earning potential is strong. At $90,000 a year, average wages are second only to chemical engineers. For those seeking experience in software engineering while in school, contributing to open source projects, interning, and entering programming contests are recommended.

A few weeks ago [in early 2011], the IBM-built supercomputer named Watson made worldwide headlines by beating several human contestants on the game show, Jeopardy!. It's a feat that would not have been possible without the software engineers behind the scenes. [*Editor's Note: On Monday, 28 February, physicist and Congressman Rush Holt (D-N.J.) saved face for humans by topping Watson in the first of three rounds of an exhibition Jeopardy! match.*]

"Software engineering is one of the fastest growing fields in the world today," says Ben Amaba, worldwide executive for IBM Complex Systems. "What we're seeing across all other disciplines is that software is becoming an invisible thread tying all disciplines together. Software is now embedded in almost all devices, mechanical devices all talk with each other, and developing products using software is faster and poses fewer risks than physical prototyping."

Why Software Engineering Is Important

Software engineering was recently dubbed the best job of 2011 by career site Career Cast, and magazines like *Forbes* and *Fortune* have also extolled the virtues and importance of the field. Heck, even toy company Mattel recently introduced Computer Engineer Barbie to help inspire young girls into the profession.

That doesn't mean there are jobs for everybody, but the prospects are good for software engineers, and they have one of the lowest levels of joblessness among engineering professions.

So why are these employees so valuable? Look no further than the often-cited Standish Group "Chaos" reports, which most recently (2009) found that only 32% of software projects are, in their terms, "successful." The Standish report found that 44% of software projects were "challenged," usually involving cost over-runs and late delivery, and a full 24% of projects failed. Since companies often can't afford these costly delays or failures, engineers who operate by a set of standard development principles, such as those defined in the Software Engineering Body of Knowledge (SWEBOK), can help keep costs down and products flowing out the door.

"Software engineers can also have higher innovation rates," says Amaba, "because they aren't tied to the physical world. Their only constraint is time. Other areas are more limited by materials and manpower."

The Field

According to the Bureau of Labor Statistics (BLS), the number of employed software engineers has grown more than 25 percent in the past decade, from 745,000 in 2001 to 1,206,000 in 2010. The earning potential for software engineers is also strong, with both computer systems and applications software engineers averaging more than $90,000 in annual wages in 2009, according to BLS data. Among all other engineering fields, only chemical engineers averaged higher annual wages in 2009 at just over $96,000.

That doesn't mean there are jobs for everybody, but the prospects are good for software engineers, and they have one of the lowest levels of joblessness among engineering professions. According to the BLS, software engineering unemployment was 4.6% in 2010, compared to 5.4% for electrical engineers.

Chris Ruoff, Sr. Manager of Sales and Channel Development for the IEEE [Institute of Electrical and Electronic Engineers] Computer Society points out that professional certifications, like the IEEE Computer Society's Certified Software Development Associate and Certified Software Development Professional, are now becoming recommended or even required by companies seeking to hire software engineers. "More and more organizations are recognizing the benefit of hiring someone who has a solid foundation in software engineering and provides a lower risk as a new hire." The SWEBOK Guide is used world-wide in academia and in industry and provides a great resource to build this foundation.

What Employers Are Looking For

"Software engineers need good communication skills, both spoken and written," says Amaba. "They need an analytical capability, and they need to be able to manage a project from end to end while working well with their colleagues." He says employees also need to be able to keep up with rapidly changing technologies. "Also, the more they know about the social sciences, physical sciences and mathematical sciences, the better they will be able to succeed."

[Software engineers] need to be able to work on a project from A to Z and solve problems at every level, not just be able to write code.

"As a hiring manager, I'm looking for candidates to show me two things: that they are smart and can get things done," says Jensen Crawford, director of engineering for Fetch Technologies. "The former includes being able to communicate about, analyze and solve problems. The latter is being able to deliver those solutions." If you're looking for experience, Crawford recommends a few steps, especially for anyone who is still in school: "Contribute to open source projects, work as an intern, and enter programming contests," he says. "Having proof that you delivered software will give you a real advantage over other candidates."

Software engineering will be of great need in a number of fields in the coming years, says Bruce Douglas, chief evangelist for IBM Rational. A few examples include probability and statistics, environmental engineering, economics, ethics, and electric vehicle mechanics. "Software engineers with knowledge and fundamentals on electric vehicles will be in better position to create complex battery systems, electric drive units and cabin electronics," he says.

"What we have found is you need product-oriented people," says Arvind Srinivasan, chief technology officer and co-founder of ZL Technologies. "They need to be able to work on a project from A to Z and solve problems at every level, not just be able to write code. We hire people with a mathematical background and a strong engineering sense." Srinivasan says one of the main things he wants to see from a job candidate is if they have already shipped a product. "If not, it doesn't matter how well you write code."

A software engineer is the best support engineer, says Srinivasan. "They can support what they write, find a problem and fix it. They have a good sense of what the customer is thinking and can respond to customer requirements. They also understand the quality assurance process and make sure that products are of high value."

All of the people I spoke with this article discussed how important software engineering is not just for today, but for the future. "Software engineering is going to change the world," says Amaba. "It's becoming embedded in the devices we all use every day." Srinivasan agrees: "Software engineering is the nuts and bolts for the entire future. You need software for everything these days. It's deeper than deep. I think it's going to become the new English."

5

Fewer Youths Are Seeking Jobs in Agriculture

Joseph Cress

Joseph Cress is a journalist at the Sentinel *based in Carlisle, Pennsylvania.*

Because of the growing disconnect between society and agriculture, fewer young people are pursuing jobs in farming. High school students interested in agriculture as a career choice are scarce, and current farm operators are aging. This disconnect is attributed to technological advances: only 1.5 to 2 percent of America's population live on farms today, resulting in less awareness and appreciation of where food comes from. In fact, working in agriculture is looked down upon as less challenging, less skilled, and less profitable than other fields. However, through certification obtained right out of high school, workers in farming and related trades can earn good incomes without the expense or debt of a college education.

A disconnect exists between society and agriculture, which experts say is rooted in a lack of appreciation for what it takes to bring food from the farm to the fork.

One result of that disconnect has been fewer young people entering farming at a time when the average age of a principal operator in Cumberland County is 54, according to the National Agricultural Statistics Service in Harrisburg.

"We are getting so removed from our food supply," said Nathan Repetz, 18, president of the Pennsylvania State 4-H Council. "Once you are removed from anything for too long, you start to lose track of it."

Family ties have kept the New Cumberland teen connected to agriculture. Both his mother and grandmother were active in 4-H, a youth development program. His grandfather Charles Itle worked the Pennsylvania Farm Show for 30 years and once served as its livestock manager.

But in the Cedar Cliff High School Class of 2013, Repetz was more the exception than the rule. He was the only graduate known by the guidance counselor to be pursuing agriculture as a career choice. For Repetz, the desire to help the public reconnect to the farm is driving his goal to earn a degree in agricultural and extension education from Penn State University. He is a freshman at the Altoona campus.

"The industry is taking a hit because people do not appreciate it enough," Repetz said of agriculture. "People do not give it enough credit."

Change over Time

This disconnect from farming was brought about by cultural changes made over time.

Being able to do more with less people freed up many growing up on farms to explore other career fields.

When Cumberland County was first settled, the majority of its population had close ties to agriculture and more of an awareness of what went into production.

As industries outside agriculture began to emerge, the technology of farming improved, resulting in greater efficiency and less of a demand for labor, said Sherisa Nailor, an agriculture teacher at Big Spring High School.

Being able to do more with less people freed up many growing up on farms to explore other career fields, Nailor said. She added some of those who went to college came back with new ideas and methods of farming that set them at odds with the older generation of farmers uncomfortable with change.

Children raised on farms often live with the financial struggles of trying to keep a family operation profitable, Repetz said. They see what their parents have to deal with and wonder if they want to put themselves through it. Some opt out entirely rather than carry on the farm tradition through the next generation.

Fewer people working the farm means less awareness of agriculture in society-at-large.

"It goes all the way down to people who have no idea where their food comes from," Repetz said. "I want to bring awareness to the number one industry in Pennsylvania—and it can be argued the most important industry to civilization."

The concern Nailor and other experts have is whether the trend has reached the point where society needs to worry about who is going to produce food for future generations. Today, only 1.5 to 2 percent of the American population lives on a farm, said Dave Swartz, county director of the Penn State Cooperative Extension.

Perspective

One result of this disconnect has been a change in the way the current generation and society in general views farmers.

All too often, people look down upon those who work the land as less-skilled, less-smart and less-driven, when the work is actually more technical and complex than credited, Repetz said.

"It is not appealing by society to do hard work in the sun or the dirt," he said.

There is a misconception that a young person cannot make as much money in farming as they could with a white collar job, said Tyler Brown, 17, a senior at Cumberland Valley High School and a member of the local FFA chapter.

"If you get into farming and pull the right ties, you can be successful and make a lot of money," Tyler said. "People want to get more money for doing the least amount of work possible, where in farming you can get more money, but you work really hard.

"I don't think agriculture is understood at all," he added. "Everything you have in everyday life comes from farming. People take it for granted."

The pressure on youth not to pursue farming and other hands-on jobs comes more from outside influences like society, parents and guidance counselors, rather than the students themselves.

Local farmer Bert Myers said society needs to get away from the idea that a young person needs a college education and a white collar job to be successful. He agreed that the perception exists among some in society that the hard work that goes into farming does not necessarily equate to tangible rewards.

His advice to young people is to pursue a path where they feel productive and fulfilled and where they are helping the community.

As a teacher, Nailor said he believes the pressure on youth not to pursue farming and other hands-on jobs comes more from outside influences like society, parents and guidance counselors, rather than the students themselves.

"A college education is great. . . . We will never discourage it especially if that is what the career will call for," Nailor said.

She added, however, that students who go into the trades and farming can earn a decent living with a certification right out of school without having to be in debt, paying off student loans.

"The biggest thing we can do as a culture is just learn how to value good food," said Brooks Miller, a Perry County farmer. "If we learn how to value food, people would be willing to pay more for it. If nobody values food than why would you want to be a producer of it?"

6

College Degrees Will Be Valuable for the Jobs of the Future

Pew Research Center

Pew Research Center is a nonpartisan think tank that conducts public opinion polling, demographic research, media content analysis, and other empirical social science research.

With soaring student debt and high unemployment, the value of a college education is now being questioned. However, young college graduates are outperforming their peers on nearly all measures of economic well-being and career attainment. Based on an analysis of data from the US Census Bureau, millennials with college degrees working full-time earn $17,500 more than those with only high school diplomas. In addition, these college graduates are more likely to have jobs (89 percent versus 82 percent) and less likely to be jobless (3.8 percent versus 12.2 percent). Furthermore, a survey shows that a high majority of college graduates believe that the costs of college will pay off: 72 percent report that it already has and 17 percent state that it will in the future.

For those who question the value of college in this era of soaring student debt and high unemployment, the attitudes and experiences of today's young adults—members of the so-called Millennial generation—provide a compelling answer. On virtually every measure of economic well-being and career attainment—from personal earnings to job satisfaction to the share employed full time—young college graduates are outperforming their peers with less education. And when today's young adults are compared with previous generations, the disparity in economic outcomes between college graduates and those with a high school diploma or less formal schooling has never been greater in the modern era.

These assessments are based on findings from a new nationally representative Pew Research Center survey of 2,002 adults supplemented by a Pew Research analysis of economic data from the U.S. Census Bureau.

The economic analysis finds that Millennial college graduates ages 25 to 32 who are working full time earn more annually—about $17,500 more—than employed young adults holding only a high school diploma. The pay gap was significantly smaller in previous generations. College-educated Millennials also are more likely to be employed full time than their less-educated counterparts (89% vs. 82%) and significantly less likely to be unemployed (3.8% vs. 12.2%).

Turning to attitudes toward work, employed Millennial college graduates are more likely than their peers with a high school diploma or less education to say their job is a career or a steppingstone to a career (86% vs. 57%). In contrast, Millennials with a high school diploma or less are about three times as likely as college graduates to say their work is "just a job to get [them] by" (42% vs. 14%).

The survey and economic analysis consistently find that college graduates regardless of generation are doing better than those with less education.

The survey also finds that among employed Millennials, college graduates are significantly more likely than those without any college experience to say that their education has been "very useful" in preparing them for work and a career (46% vs. 31%). And these better educated young adults are more likely to say they have the necessary education and training to advance in their careers (63% vs. 41%).

But do these benefits outweigh the financial burden imposed by four or more years of college? Among Millennials ages 25 to 32, the answer is clearly yes: About nine-in-ten with at least a bachelor's degree say college has already paid off (72%) or will pay off in the future (17%). Even among the two-thirds of college-educated Millennials who borrowed money to pay for their schooling, about nine-in-ten (86%) say their degrees have been worth it or expect that they will be in the future.

The Benefits Are Not Limited to Millennials

Of course, the economic and career benefits of a college degree are not limited to Millennials. Overall, the survey and economic analysis consistently find that college graduates regardless of generation are doing better than those with less education.

But the Pew Research study also finds that on some key measures, the largest and most striking disparities between college graduates and those with less education surface in the Millennial generation.

For example, in 1979 when the first wave of Baby Boomers were the same age that Millennials are today, the typical high school graduate earned about three-quarters (77%) of what a college graduate made. Today, Millennials with only a high school diploma earn 62% of what the typical college graduate earns.

To be sure, the Great Recession and the subsequent slow recovery hit the Millennial generation particularly hard. Neither college graduates nor those with less education were spared. On some key measures such as the percentage who are unemployed or the share living in poverty, this generation of college-educated adults is faring worse than Gen Xers, Baby Boomers or members of the Silent generation when they were in their mid-20s and early 30s.

But today's high school graduates are doing even worse, both in comparison to their college-educated peers and when measured against other generations of high school graduates at a similar point in their lives.

For example, among those ages 25 to 32, fully 22% with only a high school diploma are living in poverty, compared with 6% of today's college-educated young adults. In contrast, only 7% of Baby Boomers who had only a high school diploma were in poverty in 1979 when they were in their late 20s and early 30s.

To examine the value of education in today's job market, the Pew Research Center drew from two complementary data sources. The first is a nationally representative survey conducted Oct. 7-27, 2013, of 2,002 adults, including 630 Millennials ages 25-32, the age at which most of these young adults will have completed their formal education and started their working lives. This survey captured the views of today's adults toward their education, their job and their experiences in the workforce.

Today's Millennials are the best-educated generation in history; fully a third (34%) have at least a bachelor's degree.

To measure how the economic outcomes of older Millennials compare with those of other generations at a comparable age, the Pew Research demographic analysis drew from data collected in the government's Current Population Survey [CPS]. The CPS is a large-sample survey that has been conducted monthly by the U.S. Census Bureau for more than six decades.

Specifically, Pew analysts examined CPS data collected last year [2013] among 25- to 32-year-olds and then examined data among 25- to 32-year-olds in four earlier years: Silents in 1965 (ages 68 to 85 at the time of the Pew Research survey and Current Population Survey); the first or "early" wave of Baby Boomers in 1979 (ages 59 to 67 in 2013), the younger or "late" wave of Baby Boomers in 1986 (ages 49 to 58 in 2013) and Gen Xers in 1995 (ages 33 to 48 in 2013).

The Rise of the College Graduate

Today's Millennials are the best-educated generation in history; fully a third (34%) have at least a bachelor's degree. In contrast, only 13% of 25- to 32-year-olds in 1965—the Silent generation—had a college degree, a proportion that increased to 24% in the late 1970s and 1980s when Boomers were young adults. In contrast, the proportion with a high school diploma has declined from 43% in 1965 to barely a quarter (26%) today.

At the same time the share of college graduates has grown, the value of their degrees has increased. Between 1965 and last year, the median annual earnings of 25- to 32-year-olds with a college degree grew from $38,833 to $45,500 in 2012 dollars, nearly a $7,000 increase.

Taken together, these two facts—the growing economic return to a college degree and the larger share of college graduates in the Millennial generation—might suggest that the Millennial generation should be earning more than earlier generations of young adults.

But they're not. The overall median earnings of today's Millennials ($35,000) aren't much different than the earnings of early Boomers ($34,883) or Gen Xers ($32,173) and only somewhat higher than Silents ($30,982) at comparable ages.

The Declining Value of a High School Diploma

The explanation for this puzzling finding lies in another major economic trend reshaping the economic landscape: The dramatic decline in the value of a high school education. While earnings of those with a college degree rose, the typical high school graduate's earnings fell by more than $3,000, from $31,384 in 1965 to $28,000 in 2013. This decline, the Pew Research analysis found, has been large enough to nearly offset the gains of college graduates.

The steadily widening earnings gap by educational attainment is further highlighted when the analysis shifts to track the difference over time in median earnings of college graduates versus those with a high school diploma.

In 1965, young college graduates earned $7,499 more than those with a high school diploma. But the earnings gap by educational attainment has steadily widened since then, and today it has more than doubled to $17,500 among Millennials ages 25 to 32.

Other Labor Market Outcomes

To be sure, the Great Recession and painfully slow recovery have taken their toll on the Millennial generation, including the college-educated.

The unemployment rate for Millennials with a college degree is more than double the rate for college-educated Silents in 1965. . . . But the unemployment rate for Millennials with only a high school diploma is even higher.

Young college graduates are having more difficulty landing work than earlier cohorts. They are more likely to be unemployed and have to search longer for a job than earlier generations of young adults.

But the picture is consistently bleaker for less-educated workers: On a range of measures, they not only fare worse than the college-educated, but they are doing worse than earlier generations at a similar age.

For example, the unemployment rate for Millennials with a college degree is more than double the rate for college-educated Silents in 1965 (3.8% vs. 1.4%). But the unemployment rate for Millennials with only a high school diploma is even higher: 12.2%, or more than 8 percentage points more than for college graduates and almost triple the unemployment rate of Silents with a high school diploma in 1965.

The same pattern resurfaces when the measure shifts to the length of time the typical job seeker spends looking for work. In 2013 the average unemployed college-educated Millennial had been looking for work for 27 weeks—more than double the time it took an unemployed college-educated 25- to 32-year-old in 1979 to get a job (12 weeks). Again, today's young high school graduates fare worse on this measure than the college-educated or their peers in earlier generations. According to the analysis, Millennial high school graduates spend, on average, four weeks longer looking for work than college graduates (31 weeks vs. 27 weeks) and more than twice as long as similarly educated early Boomers did in 1979 (12 weeks).

Similarly, in terms of hours worked, likelihood of full-time employment and overall wealth, today's young college graduates fare worse than their peers in earlier generations. But again, Millennials without a college degree fare worse, not only in comparison to their college-educated contemporaries but also when compared with similarly educated young adults in earlier generations.

The Value of a College Major

As the previous sections show, having a college degree is helpful in today's job market. But depending on their major field of study, some are more relevant on the job than others, the Pew Research survey finds.

To measure the value of their college studies, all college graduates were asked their major or, if they held a graduate or professional degree, their field of study. Overall, 37% say they were social science, liberal arts or education majors, a third (33%) say they studied a branch of science or engineering and a quarter (26%) majored in business. The remainder said they were studying or training for a vocational occupation.

Overall, those who studied science or engineering are the most likely to say that their current job is "very closely" related to their college or graduate field of study (60% vs. 43% for both social science, liberal arts or education majors and business majors).

At the same time, those who majored in science or engineering are less likely than social science, liberal arts or education majors to say in response to another survey question that they should have chosen a different major as an undergraduate to better prepare them for the job they wanted.

According to the survey, only about a quarter of science and engineering majors regretted their decision (24%), compared with 33% of those whose degree is in social science, liberal arts or education. Some 28% of business majors say they would have been better prepared for the job they wanted if they had chosen a different major. (Overall, the survey found that 29% say they should have chosen a different major to better prepare them for their ideal job.)

Major Regrets

In addition to selecting a different major, the Pew Research survey asked college graduates whether, while still in school, they could have better prepared for the type of job they wanted by gaining more work experience, studying harder or beginning their job search earlier.

About three-quarters of all college graduates say taking at least one of those four steps would have enhanced their chances to land their ideal job. Leading the should-have-done list: getting more work experience while still in school. Half say taking this step would have put them in a better position to get the kind of job they wanted. About four-in-ten (38%) regret not studying harder, while three-in-ten say they should have started looking for a job sooner (30%) or picked a different major (29%).

When analyzed together, the survey suggests that, among these items tested, only about a quarter (26%) of all college graduates have no regrets, while 21% say they should have done at least three or all four things differently while in college to enhance their chances for a job they wanted.

The survey also found that Millennials are more likely than Boomers to have multiple regrets about their college days. Three-in-ten (31%) of all Millennials and 17% of Boomers say they should have done three or all four things differently in order to prepare themselves for the job they wanted. Some 22% of Gen Xers say the same.

A Matter of Degrees

Anne Kim

Based in Washington, DC, Anne Kim is a writer and senior fellow at the Progressive Policy Institute.

Skills-based credentials for better paying jobs are emerging in numerous industries as an alternative to traditional college degrees. For employers, a post-secondary education does not guarantee that a job candidate possesses the work habits and skills to perform. For students, earning a degree is becoming too expensive and time-consuming, especially for those who work full-time and have families. Industries such as manufacturing are developing standardized credentialing systems in which workers earn credentials through testing and skills assessment for career advancement. Also, businesses are partnering with colleges and universities to allow workers to earn academic units toward traditional degrees while on the job. The emphasis on skills-based credentials fuels the debate over the value of a traditional college degree.

Imagine you're a twenty-five-year-old high school graduate. You're married, you have two kids, you work full-time as an office manager for a local company. You've taken a few classes at your community college nearby but haven't finished your degree. With a family to raise, you want to earn more money, perhaps working with computers, your passion. You think of yourself as the creative type, and your friends tell you there's a good living to be made in Web design. What do you do?

One option is to enroll at DeVry University, where an associate's degree in Web design will cost you roughly $39,000 in tuition and five full semesters—at least two years—of class time. You could also go back to your local community college and pay much less, about $2,000, for an eight-course certificate in Web design basics.

Or you could simply log on to openbadges.org, and, from the comfort of your home, learn what you need to know, at your own pace—for free.

Web browser maker Mozilla launched openbadges.org in 2011 to promote what they call "digital badges" to anyone who can demonstrate that they've mastered a specific skill. Much like Boy Scout merit badges, participants can earn their way up the badge ladder. Aspiring Web designers, for example, can earn a badge as a "Code Whisperer," an "Editor," a "Div Master," or a "Super Styler," depending on their ability to demonstrate their coding skills and to build their own Web projects. At the top are the "HTML Basic" and "I am a Webmaker" badges, stepping stones for becoming the Eagle Scout of the Mozilla digital badge world: a "Mozilla Webmaker Master."

From an employer's perspective, traditional degrees aren't always all that useful. . . . They don't reveal much about an applicant's actual skills.

Each badge earned gets you an icon to display on your digital resume or as part of your online profile, which you can show to prospective employers. More than 1,000 groups and employers, including NASA, Disney-Pixar, the Smithsonian Institution, the New York City Department of Education, and Microsoft, are now offering or honoring badges recognizing a wide variety of skills. At the annual summit of the Clinton Global Initiative this summer, former President Bill Clinton endorsed the idea of badging and urged more employers to participate.

While badges are gaining steam, they are actually just one example of many new so-called skills-based credentials that are cropping up in different industries—from Web design to retail to manufacturing—thanks to employers' and students' growing disenchantment with traditional college degrees.

From an employer's perspective, traditional degrees aren't always all that useful, even though most jobs today require the high level of skills that post-secondary education is supposed to confer. While degrees serve as a kind of baseline measure of a job candidate's reliability—this person showed up for class (most of the time) for X number of years—they don't reveal much about an applicant's actual skills. Because they really only measure the amount of time a student has spent in a classroom, rather than the skills a student has acquired, degrees confer little beyond the selectivity of the college that granted them.

From the students' perspective, earning a college degree is increasingly prohibitively expensive. It's also often impossibly time-consuming, especially for the growing number of prospective students who are also trying to juggle family and a full-time job. But as long as traditional degrees are the only admission ticket to better-paying jobs, people with aspirations, who often have valuable on-the-job skill sets but no degree to prove it, can find themselves unable to move up in life.

With all this in mind, a new movement has arisen that is championing alternative avenues to credentials and traditional college degrees. In some cases, companies are bypassing traditional higher education entirely by creating new credentialing systems from scratch, like those Mozilla badges. In other cases, companies have begun partnering with traditional institutions of higher education, such as community colleges or local four-year universities, that are willing to offer their workers college credit for the skills they learn on the job.

Ultimately, these innovations could be a significant boon to students. Particularly for those at the bottom of the economic ladder, the benefit could be better access to cheaper and faster post-secondary education—a must in the changing job market. But these innovations could also threaten the business model of traditional colleges and universities that are unwilling to adapt.

As the senior vice president for the nonprofit Manufacturing Institute, Brent Weil hears complaints from his member companies all the time. When he asks them how they find new workers to hire, the top of the list is word of mouth and the second is for-profit staffing agencies. At the bottom of the list, "somewhere near the margin of error," he says, is the current system of higher education, which, he argues, fails to produce enough qualified graduates.

In the past two years, more than 84,000 manufacturing workers have earned certifications under the new system, and the industry's goal is to issue at least 500,000 by 2016.

In its 2011 "skills gap" report, the institute claimed that as many as 600,000 jobs were going unfilled due to a shortage of workers with the right skills, especially the higher-order skills that are increasingly a must in technology-driven, advanced manufacturing. In addition to specific skills such as precision machining, manufacturers say they need people who can work in teams, solve problems, and communicate with their colleagues, as well as simply show up on time. In theory, a certificate or degree from, say, a community college, should be a guarantee that a person has gained these work habits and thinking skills. In practice, too often, it is not.

Frustrated by this state of affairs, the manufacturing industry began developing its own system of industry-approved credentials for prospective employees. In 2011, the Manufacturing Institute unveiled a pyramid of "stackable credentials" that workers can collect in the same way that budding Web-masters can earn a progression of badges from Mozilla.

At the bottom of the pyramid is a basic credential—the National Career Readiness Certificate developed by the ACT testing service—attesting to the core workplace skills, such as critical thinking and teamwork, that every worker is expected to have. At the top are a variety of "skills certifications," also organized by increasing levels of knowledge, that workers can earn in specific jobs such as machining, welding, construction, and automation.

"Machining Level I," for example, qualifies a worker for entry-level jobs, while "Machining Level III" would put someone in the running for the highest-paid and most advanced work—with a potential salary of up to $80,000. In the past two years, more than 84,000 manufacturing workers have earned certifications under the new system, and the industry's goal is to issue at least 500,000 by 2016.

As with badges, the new system standardizes the skill sets required by manufacturing into an organized system that the entire industry has agreed to recognize. In the past, workers and employers had to pick through as many as 450 different certificates of varying quality, offered by a slew of industry trade groups, many of whose revenues were based on the fees collected from offering credentials, as well as by community and for-profit colleges of dubious merit (think [actor] Sally Struthers promising on late-night TV that you, too, could become a mechanic by mail).

Under the new system, each industry-endorsed credential indicates a defined set of skills and is issued only by accredited providers. To earn a credential, workers must pass both a standardized written test and a practical skills assessment (for example, building a part). Like the euro, which replaced the lira, franc, drachma, and so on, the new credentials are intended to be the industry's common currency.

As a result, Weil says, the new credentials provide both portability and precision about a worker's or job applicant's skills. The result is a market value "above and beyond college." In fact, he says, "in some cases, employers prefer certification over a two-year degree."

The potential for anyone to earn credentials through a variety of means could especially benefit older, displaced, or disadvantaged workers for whom traditional education is not an option.

Moreover, these credentials can be earned through multiple pathways, not just by going to school. Current workers, for example, can apply for certifications based on skills they've learned or are learning on the job (and thus have a portable credential they can take elsewhere, which they didn't have before).

Workers can also pick up skills in apprenticeship programs organized by the Department of Labor, company training courses, and industry-sponsored workshops, and, of course, in school. The industry-endorsed National Institute for Metalworking Skills, for example, accredits dozens of institutions across the country that are teaching the skills necessary to get an industry credential, including career and technical schools, military bases, job corps centers, and traditional colleges. Pennsylvania's Lehigh Career and Technical Institute, for example, is one of roughly forty schools nationwide that now specialize in teaching to industry standards in fields like laboratory engineering and "computer numerical controlled" technology, a form of high-tech machining.

The potential for anyone to earn credentials through a variety of means could especially benefit older, displaced, or disadvantaged workers for whom traditional education is not an option. This is a major reason why the White House and several foundations have championed the manufacturers' efforts.

At the Dunwoody College of Technology in Minneapolis, for example, prospective workers can take part in a twenty-four-week accelerated credentialing program as part of the Manufacturing Institute's Right Skills Now Initiative, geared toward unemployed, displaced, and low-skilled workers. Participants in this program spend eighteen weeks in the classroom learning computer numerical controlled technology followed by a six-week paid internship. At the end of the program, students earn a certificate from Dunwoody, one semester of credit toward an associate's degree in machine tool technology, and, if they pass the tests, four professional certifications from the National Institute for Metalworking Skills.

The manufacturers' new system of credentialing has turned out to be the tip of the spear in a broader industry push around alternative credentials and the recognition of skills. In the last couple of years, the energy, construction, and transportation sectors have begun following the manufacturers' lead; all are currently working to develop and offer their own industry-specific credentials with the help of such standards-setting bodies as the American National Standards Institute.

Other industries, such as retail and fast food, have taken a different tack. Instead of coming up with their own credentialing system, they are working to persuade colleges to convert the skills their workers acquire on the job into traditional academic units that they can accumulate to earn a traditional college degree. In this case, the "badge" is college credit.

Many retail workers are learning many of the same skills they would otherwise be learning in college.

Walmart, for example, announced a new work-for-credits partnership with the online American Public University (APU) in 2010 that provides its employees with college credit for work experience. Roughly 100 different positions qualify for the program, including cashiers, store managers, photo technicians, and inventory supervisors. To get the credit, full-time workers have to be on the job for at least one year, get good performance reviews, and take part in in-house trainings. Karan Powell, APU's provost, says approximately 5,000 Walmart employees nationwide are now enrolled in the program.

Walmart employee Henry Jordan used this program to earn his bachelor's degree in management online from APU this past summer. Jordan started out in Walmart's pet department and rose through the ranks to senior management. His years at Walmart translated into thirty credits at APU, which shaved the equivalent of one full-time year off his course work.

He says this work-for-credit program is the only way he could have gone back to school. "There are lots of people like me who are taking care of families, raising kids, and who have to work," he said, adding that in his experience many retail workers are learning many of the same skills they would otherwise be learning in college. As a store manager, for example, Jordan said he was essentially running a multimillion-dollar business, with responsibility for personnel, marketing, managing inventory, and environmental and legal compliance, as well as keeping an eye on the books.

APU's Powell said that figuring out which jobs and skills deserved college credit was a painstaking and complex process that involved mapping the skills learned in a particular job against the objectives of a particular class. "We knew it would get a lot of scrutiny, so we went above and beyond," Powell said.

This idea of finding new pathways toward higher education isn't entirely novel. In fact, the National Career Readiness Certificate at the foundation of the manufacturers' credentialing system is part of the WorkKeys skills assessment system first developed by ACT in 1992. The nontraditional work-for-credit programs, like Walmart's partnership with APU, were preceded by the nonprofit online Western Governors University, which since 1999 has pioneered the concepts of providing college credit for work skills and focusing on competency versus class time. This involves carefully testing students to see what knowledge and skills they have already picked up in school or at work and then teaching them only the extra information and capacities they'll need to perform certain professional jobs that Western Governors confers degrees in— human resource management, say, or network administration.

Traditionally, employers have often been reluctant to invest a great deal in training their employees for fear that the investment will be lost if a newly up-skilled employee goes to work for the company's competitor. But the explosion of industry interest in these nontraditional avenues of training is evidence that to an extent the calculation is changing.

Yes, some employees will seek greener pastures, but offering ways to earn credentials and degrees also turns out to be a great tool for recruiting and retaining the best people, say representatives from both the manufacturing and retail sectors. Industry-approved credentialing programs save companies money by allowing them to cherry-pick people with exactly the skills they need, rather than spending money on recruiting and training people who may not work out. It also helps improve their respective industries' images if they are perceived as dirty and dangerous, or simply low-skilled.

So long as college costs and student debt are spiraling upward, credentialing advocates say the balance should tip toward more pragmatic aims for higher education.

Peg Walton, senior director for workforce readiness at Corporate Voices for Working Families, says many businesses across the country are clamoring to get college credit for their workers, primarily through partnerships with colleges similar to the one between Walmart and APU. Starbucks, for example, launched Starbucks U, where workers can get college credit from the City University of Seattle for completing such in-house trainings as Barista 100 and Barista Basics. And Jiffy Lube workers can now get credit from the University of Maryland University College for trainings from Jiffy Lube University. UPS and energy giant AREVA have also launched partnerships to convert work skills into college credit.

Whatever the motivations, escalating industry interest in alternative credentials is feeding a larger debate about the very purpose of a college degree—what it should measure and what it should mean. Should colleges produce graduates ready to work? Or should their goal be to produce well-rounded citizens, however that may be defined? Take liberal arts colleges, for example. Liberal arts majors earn an average of $31,000 a year when they first graduate, according to the Georgetown University Center on Education and the Workforce, even though their degrees have likely cost at least three times that much. Are those colleges failing their students? Or are they providing value that's not economically transferable? Is that worth it?

So long as college costs and student debt are spiraling upward, credentialing advocates say the balance should tip toward more pragmatic aims for higher education. "People go to college because they want to work," Walton of Corporate Voices says simply.

Emily DeRocco, who served in the Department of Labor as the assistant secretary for employment and training under President George W. Bush and is now the principal of the consulting firm E3, agrees. She hopes the push toward skills-based credentials will act as a "wedge" forcing traditional institutions of higher education to consider new ways of thinking about their industry. In particular, she hopes higher education will embrace competency-based education, where what matters is a student's mastery of specific skills, not the amount of time they spend in class or the alleged prestige of their school. Under a competency-based model, community college graduates could potentially be on equal footing with Harvard MBAs [Master of Business Administration].

Parminder Jassal, the incoming executive director of the ACT Foundation, says competency-based credentials would especially benefit young, low-income, or adult learners, for whom a traditional path to a college degree is impractical.

More traditional four-year institutions are welcoming tighter partnerships with industry and acknowledging industry's needs for specific skills in shaping course work.

Jassal points out that much of the K-12 world has already embraced competency-based education—the Common Core State Standards currently being rolled out in most of the nation's schools are the most obvious example. The Obama administration has also championed the idea.

And, if you think about it, it's not outside the mold of traditional education, says DeRocco. Much of graduate and professional education, including medicine and law, is already geared toward occupational skills, not general knowledge.

In the meantime, students in traditional higher education settings, like community colleges and four-year universities, are already benefiting from the influence of industry's push to make higher education more focused on skills. For one thing, more traditional four-year institutions are welcoming tighter partnerships with industry and acknowledging industry's needs for specific skills in shaping course work.

The Maryland Cybersecurity Center, launched by the University of Maryland at College Park in 2010, boasts partnerships with more than a dozen companies, including Northrop Grumman, SAIC, and Google. A new honors program starting this fall was the product of a $1.1 million investment by Northrop Grumman and comes with a paid internship opportunity for students—an attractive feature. . . .

Jan Klevis, the director of post-secondary and workforce education at Pennsylvania's Lehigh Institute, envisions a "seamless pathway" between work and school that is the ultimate result of the credentialing movement. She imagines working adults having the opportunity to attend school part-time while earning credentials that are not only valuable within an industry but can later be converted into college credit. Under this system, she says, "you can get a four-year degree for under $10,000."

The prototype of this future student might be forty-six-year-old Joe Weischedel. As a professional truck driver, Weis-chedel spent two decades hauling everything from produce to chemicals up and down the East Coast and across the country. On his longest hauls, he's spent as much as four weeks away from home. After stints in community college as well as Temple University in Philadelphia, Weischedel joined the Army for four years and served as a combat medic. Around 2000, he tried college again with a few online classes at the University of Maryland and the University of Phoenix but ended up dropping out.

In 2010, he resumed the college education he had abandoned years earlier and enrolled online at APU. After receiving college credit for the skills he picked up in the military, it took him two years to earn his degree, taking two classes at a time and studying (while sometimes attending classes online) in hotel rooms on the road. This summer, he graduated with a bachelor's degree, with honors, in transportation and logistics management. He also earned a professional certification from the American Society of Transportation and Logistics.

Today, Weischedel is looking at senior logistics management jobs that could quadruple his current salary driving trucks. "I had the practical experience, but I didn't have the paper," he said. "There was a ceiling before, but now I've broken through."

Science and Math Education Will Provide Job Opportunities and Security

David Langdon et al.

David Langdon coauthored the following viewpoint with George McKittrick, David Beede, Beethika Khan, and Mark Doms, all of whom are economists in the Office of the Chief Economist of the US Department of Commerce's Economics and Statistics Administration.

Jobs in science, technology, engineering, and math (STEM) are the jobs of the future, essential to technological innovation and competing in the global economy. While STEM jobs currently comprise a small fraction of employment in the United States, they are projected to grow 17 percent from 2008 to 2019, compared to 9.8 percent for non-STEM jobs. On average, workers in STEM fields earn more than other workers regardless of education level—almost $25 an hour, or $9 more. In addition, STEM workers generally experience lower rates of joblessness. Considering these benefits, pursuing a STEM degree pays off for college graduates, and choosing a STEM career pays off for workers.

The acronym STEM is fairly specific in nature—referring to science, technology, engineering and math—however, there is no standard definition for what constitutes a STEM job. Science, technology, engineering and math positions consistently make the lists of STEM occupations, but there is less

David Langdon, George McKittrick, David Beede, Beethika Khan, and Mark Doms, "STEM: Good Jobs Now and for the Future," *ESA Issue Brief*, 03.11, July 2011.

consensus about whether to include other positions such as educators, managers, technicians, health-care professionals or social scientists. In this report, we define STEM jobs to include professional and technical support occupations in the fields of computer science and mathematics, engineering, and life and physical sciences. Three management occupations are also included because of their clear ties to STEM. Because of data limitations, education jobs are not included. Further, we elected not to include social scientists.

Our STEM list contains 50 specific occupation codes, and in 2010, there were 7.6 million workers in these jobs, or 5.5 percent of the workforce. To better put these jobs into context, we divide STEM occupations into four categories: computer and math, engineering and surveying, physical and life sciences, and STEM managerial occupations. Across all levels of educational attainment, the largest group of STEM jobs is within the computer and math fields, which account for close to half (46 percent) of all STEM employment. Second are engineering and surveying occupations with one-third of all STEM employment, while 13 percent are in the physical and life sciences, and 9 percent in STEM management jobs.

Workers in STEM occupations . . . earn more on average than their counterparts in other jobs, regardless of their educational attainment.

Parallel to our list of STEM occupations, we also identify a set of STEM undergraduate degree fields that span computer science and mathematics, engineering, and life and physical sciences. We define STEM degree holders as persons whose primary or secondary undergraduate major was in a STEM field. Following similar logic to what we used in our occupation selection, we exclude business, healthcare, and social science majors.

STEM Employment and Worker Earnings

In 2010, 7.6 million people or 1 in 18 workers held STEM jobs. Although STEM employment currently makes up only a small fraction of total U.S. employment, STEM employment grew rapidly from 2000 to 2010, increasing 7.9 percent. In contrast, employment in non-STEM jobs grew just 2.6 percent over this period. STEM jobs are projected to grow at a fast pace relative to other occupations. From 2008 to 2018, STEM jobs are expected to grow 17.0 percent compared to just 9.8 percent for non-STEM jobs.

Workers in STEM occupations also earn more on average than their counterparts in other jobs, regardless of their educational attainment. The STEM earnings differential is greatest for those with a high school diploma or less in comparison to their counterparts in a non-STEM field. On average, they earned almost $25 per hour, $9 more per hour than those in other occupations in 2010. It should be noted, however, that only about 1 out of every 10 STEM workers has a high school diploma or less. Those with graduate degrees in a STEM job earned more than $40 per hour, nearly $4.50 more per hour on average than those with non-STEM jobs.

The comparison of wage premiums raises several questions, including to what extent the STEM-earnings premium reflects other characteristics of workers, such as age, and how premiums have evolved over time. A regression analysis—which controls for a variety of demographic, geographic, and other worker characteristics—helps to address these questions. Using Current Population Survey public-use microdata for 1994–2010, we regressed the log of earnings against a standard list of characteristics that have typically been found to be related to earnings including age, marital status, race, ethnicity, region and industry.

After controlling for this set of characteristics, the earning premium diminishes somewhat. However, the fundamental result that STEM workers enjoy large earnings premiums persists, most predominantly for workers with less than a college degree. STEM earnings premiums have also shown persistence over time, and have generally increased since the mid-1990s. In 2010, workers in STEM jobs with less than a bachelor's degree enjoyed a large premium (more than 30 percent) compared with non-STEM workers with the same education level, even after taking other influences on earnings into account. The regression-based premiums in 2010 were slightly less for workers with a bachelor's (23 percent) or graduate degree (12 percent), and relatively closer to the premiums found in the simple comparison (without a regression adjustment). The overall regression-based STEM premium was 26 percent in 2010, up from 18 percent in 1994.

STEM Jobs and STEM Degrees

The analysis so far has focused on STEM jobs, but conversations about policy most often focus on STEM education. One source of information to analyze the link between STEM jobs and STEM education is the 2009 American Community Survey which collected information on college-educated individuals' undergraduate majors. When examining the relationship between STEM education and STEM jobs, the following patterns emerge.

All STEM degree holders receive an earnings premium relative to other college graduates, whether or not they end up in a STEM job.

First, a STEM degree is the typical path to a STEM job, as more than two-thirds of the 4.7 million STEM workers with a college degree has an undergraduate STEM degree. However, this does not necessarily mean that STEM workers' degrees are in the same STEM field as their jobs. For example, only 35 percent of college-educated computer and math workers have a degree in computer science or math while 27 percent majored in the physical or life sciences or engineering.

Second, in addition to STEM jobs, STEM degrees also open the door to many other career opportunities. Almost two-thirds of the 9.3 million workers with a STEM undergraduate degree work in a non-STEM job. Life and physical science majors are the STEM degree holders most likely to work in non-STEM jobs; 81 percent of these graduates work outside the STEM fields. (Note that "non-STEM" occupations include the 28 percent of graduates who work as healthcare practitioners or technicians, and the 12 percent who work in education.) In math, there is a strong pipeline into education jobs, as one-fifth of math majors go on to work in education.

As discussed above, STEM workers earn significantly more than their non-STEM counterparts, but what about the earnings of STEM degree holders who don't necessarily work in STEM jobs? Using the 2009 American Community Survey public-use microdata, calculations of the regression-adjusted earnings premium of college-educated workers with a STEM degree and/or STEM job showed that all STEM degree holders receive an earnings premium relative to other college graduates, whether or not they end up in a STEM job. Likewise, college graduates, regardless of their major, enjoy an earnings premium for having a STEM job. The earnings premium for having a STEM job or a STEM degree is quite similar, at 13 percent and 11 percent, respectively. Still, a much larger payoff tends to come when a STEM major goes on to work in a STEM job, as their earnings (all else equal) are about 20 percent higher than those of non-STEM majors working in non-STEM jobs.

STEM Joblessness

In addition to higher earnings, workers in STEM occupations on average experience lower unemployment rates than workers in other fields. The unemployment rate for STEM workers rose from 1.8 percent in 2007 to 5.5 percent in 2009 before easing to 5.3 percent in 2010. The unemployment rate for non-STEM workers rose from 4.8 percent in 2007 to 9.5 percent in 2009 and then continued to increase to almost 10 percent in 2010. STEM workers, however, are not totally immune to economic downturns, as STEM joblessness did increase during the last two recessions.

Although still relatively small in number, the STEM workforce has an outsized impact on a nation's competitiveness, economic growth, and overall standard of living.

Some of the difference in unemployment rates between STEM and non-STEM workers reflects differences in educational attainment. On balance, workers with a higher educational level tend to experience lower unemployment, and STEM workers tend to be better educated. Looking at workers with a bachelor's degree or graduate degree, one finds less of a difference in unemployment rates between STEM and non-STEM workers than for those with less education. During the latest recession, the unemployment rate for college-educated STEM workers edged above the non-STEM rate in 2009, but the rate for both groups converged to 4.7 percent in 2010. While college-educated STEM workers were less likely to be jobless than other workers during the latter part of the last two economic expansions, they were more likely to be jobless during and after the 2001 recession. The decrease in the demand for information technology workers following the Y2K efforts and the crash of the Internet dot-com bubble likely played a role.

Educational Attainment of STEM Workers

One of the more distinguishing characteristics of STEM workers is their educational attainment. More than two-thirds (68 percent) of STEM workers have a bachelor's degree or higher, compared to just under one-third (31 percent) of other workers age 16 and over. Among the four STEM occupational groups, the physical and life sciences have the highest-educated workforce, with nearly 40 percent holding a graduate degree— about double the share for computer, math and engineering jobs. Nonetheless, because STEM includes professionals as well as first-tier support jobs, we find that a number of STEM workers have less than a four-year college degree; nearly one-quarter (23 percent) have completed an associate degree or at least some college, and 9 percent have a high school diploma or less. So while it is certainly true that the majority of STEM workers tend to have at least a bachelor's degree, opportunities also exist for STEM workers with lower education levels.

STEM Careers Pay Off

The greatest advancements in our society from medicine to mechanics have come from the minds of those interested in or studied in the areas of STEM. Although still relatively small in number, the STEM workforce has an outsized impact on a nation's competitiveness, economic growth, and overall standard of living. Analysis of data from the U.S. Census Bureau's American Community Survey and Current Population Survey provide new insights into the growing STEM workforce that is central to our economic vitality. STEM jobs are the jobs of the future. They are essential for developing our technological innovation and global competitiveness.

These factors make STEM workers highly desirable to companies developing or operating on the technological forefront and extremely important to the U.S. economy, as competitive businesses are the foundation of a competitive economy. As this analysis highlights, STEM jobs should also be highly desirable to American workers. Regardless of educational attainment, entering a STEM profession is associated with higher earnings and reduced joblessness. For college graduates, there is a payoff in choosing to pursue a STEM degree, and for America's workers, an even greater payoff in choosing a STEM career.

9

Gender Gaps May Continue in Science and Math Education

Kimberly Pohl and Melissa Silverberg

Kimberly Pohl is a former senior writer for the Daily Herald *and media relations manager at Harper College. Melissa Silverberg is a staff writer at the* Daily Herald.

Despite the projected growth for jobs in science, technology, engineering, and math (STEM), young women remain the minority in college programs that prepare students for occupations in these fields. In fact, fewer female students than male students take Advanced Placement exams in calculus, chemistry, and other related subjects, and those that do score lower than men. Therefore, numerous initiatives have been launched to address the underrepresentation of women in STEM education, such as programs, workshops, and conferences that start in elementary school. Nonetheless, it remains unknown whether these efforts will attract more female students to STEM learning and careers.

Jane Halloran doesn't hesitate when asked about her future career plans.

The South Elgin teen has been certain she'll go into environmental engineering ever since her introduction as a seventh-grader to Project Lead the Way, a national, hands-on curriculum aimed at preparing students for the science, technology, engineering and math (STEM) fields.

Now, she's among 88 freshmen from across Elgin Area School District U-46 enrolled at the district's highly selective Academy of Science, Engineering and Technology housed at Bartlett High School.

In the Minority

As a girl, however, Halloran is in the minority.

Of that gifted group of academy students, just 25 are female. And of the nearly 1,000 U-46 high school students enrolled last year [2012] in Project Lead the Way, only between 200 and 250 were female.

"We know it's not an equal representation, so we're trying to make sure we get more access and participation of females in STEM classes," said Marc Hans, district coordinator of math, science, planetarium and instructional technology.

U-46's figures reflect a national trend of girls lagging behind boys when it comes to interest and participation in STEM education. According to a report released earlier this year by STEMConnector nearly 40 percent of high school boys express an interest in STEM education, compared to just 14.5 percent of girls. The gender gap, according to the report, is widening even as the number of jobs in science and engineering is expected to grow.

Fewer girls than boys take Advanced Placement exams in STEM-related subjects such as calculus or chemistry, and the girls who do take those tests earn lower scores on average than boys.

U-46 officials and school districts across the suburbs hope the persisting gender gap will shrink as initiatives targeting younger girls pay off.

Their efforts are necessary, they say, given the changing economy.

Projections from the U.S. Department of Labor show that by 2018, significant science or math training will be needed for nine out of the 10 fastest-growing jobs requiring a bachelor's degree.

Yet fewer girls than boys take Advanced Placement exams in STEM-related subjects such as calculus or chemistry, and the girls who do take those tests earn lower scores on average than boys, according to the 2010 report "Why So Few: Women in Science, Technology, Engineering and Math."

"We need STEM education because we need to prepare our students for the workforce they will enter," said Andresse St. Rose, senior researcher with the American Association of University Women and co-author of the report. "These jobs fuel innovations, they fuel the economy and they are some of the better-paying jobs out there."

To help address the underrepresentation, U-46 for the past three years has partnered with the National Alliance for Partnerships in Equity and received a Motorola Solutions Foundation grant for the purpose of engaging more female students in STEM coursework.

Engaging More Female Students

Teachers and administrators discussed the issue and the district held student focus groups to identify the causes, a key aspect of the grant.

One popular initiative to come out of that was a Saturday program for middle-school girls known as Moving Forward with STEM. During one outing last winter, students took a field trip to DeKalb and met with Latina women at the Northern Illinois University College of Engineering. Hans said 180 girls signed up for 75 spots.

The STEM academy's female students also run workshops for elementary school girls. Surveys afterward show a significant increase in the younger students' desire to take those types of classes.

"There's a huge interest from the students, and we need to make sure we can offer programming that is relevant to these young female students," Hans said. "That will build the pipeline."

Intervention as early as elementary school is key, research shows. According to the National Science Foundation, a recent study of fourth-graders showed 66 percent of girls and 68 percent of boys reported liking science. But stereotypes start to turn girls off, and by eighth grade, boys are twice as interested in STEM careers as girls.

Three years ago, Palatine-Schaumburg Township High School District 211 started an annual GEMS (Girls in Engineering, Math and Science) conference for about 150 fifth- and sixth-grade girls in its elementary feeder districts.

They learn about a variety of STEM-related professions from successful women and perform hands-on activities such as 3-D computer software modeling and forensic scientist fingerprinting. Parents also attend to learn what they can do at home.

Since the first participants aren't yet in high school, it remains to be seen whether the conference will yield results. Last year, only 84 of the 631 students enrolled in Project Lead the Way across all five District 211 high schools were female.

"We know our girls are taking rigorous courses," Assistant Superintendent for Instruction Theresa Busch said, noting that 54.7 percent of AP exams in District 211 were taken by female students. "Enticing them into male-dominated engineering is something we're working on."

In Wheeling Township Elementary District 21, middle school students participate in 12-week exploratory technology classes each year to focus on STEM topics from robotics and civil engineering to TV broadcasting and graphic design.

Opportunities Are Gender Neutral

Chief Information Officer Jason Klein said students focus on "authentic learning," or using their skills to solve real-world problems. Though District 21 doesn't target its programs specifically for girls versus boys, there have been discussions. "We hope all the kids can see that the full range of opportunities is gender neutral," he said.

Other top-ranked high schools including Stevenson also report a pretty even split among boys and girls enrolled in STEM-related classes.

Steve Wood, Stevenson's director of science, said women represent half the faculty in the school's physics and chemistry departments and lead several science clubs.

"We have a very progressive community, one that doesn't see boys as scientists and girls as something else," Wood said. "We have families that get it: There's no reason a young woman can't be a scientist or an engineer."

10

Freelancing Will Replace Traditional Employment

Brad Howarth

Brad Howarth is a journalist, author, and speaker based in Melbourne, Australia. He is the former information technology and marketing editor for the business magazine BRW.

Efforts of companies to create appealing work environments to attract and retain employees are not influencing the increasing number of workers who freelance and choose job flexibility over security. In the United States, freelancers are projected to exceed full-time workers by 2020, and it is estimated that 160 million jobs around the world can be done remotely. In Australia, the outsourcing marketplace is growing, in which the Internet is linking businesses with a global pool of skilled workers who were previously unaffordable. Nonetheless, the model has been shaped through trial and error; some freelancers misrepresent their skills, while new and aspiring ones may perform poorly.

Across Australia many employers have realised that developing and promoting an appealing working environment is an effective way to both attract and retain staff.

But even these efforts are proving insufficient in gaining the services of an increasing number of Australians, who are cashing in job security for a more flexible working lifestyle.

The exact number of Australians that are leaving full-time employment for life as a freelancer (also known as a 'soloist' in some circles) is hard to define—in part because many of Australia's freelancers are actually moonlighting after working hours.

This is seen in figures from the Australian e-commerce platform provider BigCommerce, which has found that more than half of the work done by retailers who use its software is conducted in the evening. This suggests many online retailers are working a day job and running an e-commerce site at night.

Freelance Economy

The United States in particular has seen a rapid rise in the so-called freelance economy, with freelancer numbers projected to outpace full-time workers by 2020, according to business services firm MBO Partners. The McKinsey Global Institute has also suggested that 160 million jobs—approximately 11 per cent of the world's 1.46 billion service jobs—could be carried out remotely.

While many of these freelancers work in traditional contracting arrangements, for a growing number work is facilitated through the numerous online outsourcing marketplaces, such as Freelancer.com, oDesk and Elance.

The most common jobs posted by Australian users of the site [Freelancer.com] are in the fields of graphic design, website development and content writing.

The last of these two recently merged, and Elance-oDesk now claims more than 161,000 Australian businesses registered with their services. The company has also reported growth in Australian businesses hiring through its platforms of 235 per cent over the last three years [2011 to 2014], with a combined spend of $US145 million. Elance-oDesk also reports that more than half of Australian businesses plan to hire more freelancers in 2014 than they did in 2013, based on its own research.

Rival Australian-based company Freelancer.com, which listed on the Australian Securities Exchange in late 2013, claims to provide access to 11 million freelancers around the world, with more than 4000 jobs being posted every work day.

Freelancer.com's regional manager for North American and Oceania Nikki Parker says the most common jobs posted by Australian users of the site are in the fields of graphic design, website development and content writing.

So far the service is proving most popular with small businesses, with Parker estimating that 92 per cent of users around the world work in businesses with 50 or less staff.

"Increasingly small and medium employers are engaging freelancers, because it is a cost effective and flexible way for them to grow their business without the often unaffordable expense of hiring full time, or the impossibility of finding the right employee with a specific skill set," Parker says.

"For many Australian businesses or freelancers there is a limited local client pool. However, working through an online marketplace opens up a world of opportunity, and allows Australians to work with clients and on projects that would have previously not been visible or made available to them."

Another Australian company prospering from the growth in use of freelancers is Sydney-based Airtasker, which enables people to hire freelancers for tasks ranging from handyman help to IT [information technology] support and even home or office cleaning.

Co-founder Tim Fung says the company saw the number of tasks posted double in the first quarter of this year with 120,000 registered community members, and Airtasker is now processing more than $3.5 million in annualised task revenue.

Fung says there are three distinct categories of people who are performing tasks through the site: university students, older professionals, and semi-retirees.

"Surprisingly, the most active and fastest growing segment are the semi-retirees which we believe are so successful on the platform because they have amazing experience and life skills but also the ability to share their time to help the community," Fung says.

Skills and Affordability

These services are now underpinning a number of Australian employers by delivering skills from around the world at an affordable cost.

Newcastle-based former lawyer Kim McFayden has been a long time user of online outsourcing, and is now using them to help build her new business, an online marketing service for lawyers called Lawcorner which will launch later in May.

It is not just start-ups who are taking advantage of online outsourcing.

McFayden says she uses the services for web development, writing, search engine optimisation, graphic design, video and written content creation, and virtual assistance.

"Basically my whole team is outsourced as I am a solo founder," McFayden says. "I freelance any of the competencies that I need, or don't want to be doing, or am not good at doing."

McFayden says these platforms give her access to more skills than she could access in her local market, at a more affordable cost.

It is not just start-ups who are taking advantage of online outsourcing. The managing director of Northern Territory-based talent booking agency Primetime Entertainment, Bernard Wilson, says using oDesk means he can run the Territory's largest agency with just two people.

"We spend most of our time attending to the service aspect of the business and not worrying too much about the back end, which is where oDesk comes into it," Wilson says. "I can spend more of my time with clients and less of my time doing those other things which all small business owners have to do."

Succeeding Through Trial and Error

But Wilson cautions that not all freelancers represent themselves appropriately online, and the model has only succeeded through trial and error.

"There is a lot of fear with outsourcing your business operations," he says. "But the one thing you do have to invest in is the right business systems, so you can plug in those different offshore workers in a secure and highly collaborative way."

Numerous models for organising freelancers are also emerging that aim to reduce the bumps that clients might suffer. Virtual Coworker for instance has been set up specifically to recruit and train Philippines-based workers.

Business development manager Kevin Mallen says Virtual Coworker recruits staff to meet the needs of its clients, and handles their payroll and human resources requirements.

"Essentially the staff in the Philippines become the client's employees and are working in their time zone and are in touch with them on a daily basis," Mallen says.

In the last two years the company has grown to employ 80 staff and expects to have added another 20 by early in the New Year.

He says Virtual Coworker picked the Philippines due to the quality of its university graduates.

Maureen Shelley and her business partner Dominique Antarakis run a team of freelance writers, photographers and designers under the name The Copy Collective. Their business has grown from a dozen freelancers a year ago to more than 80 today, managed by five full time staff.

Freelancers are sourced from around the world and range from university students to retirees, many of whom have multiple tertiary qualifications.

Shelley says would-be members are put through an exhaustive induction process and undertake ongoing training. In return The Copy Collective provides professional indemnity and public liability cover, as well as work. Jobs are allocated to freelancers whose skill sets are appropriate to the task, and each works at the level they want to.

"Some people earn $8000 a year with us because that's all the work they want," Shelley says. "Our top paid person gets $144,000 a year, and we have lots of people in between."

Freelancers are sourced from around the world and range from university students to retirees, many of whom have multiple tertiary qualifications. Shelley says some are home-based carers, while many are fulltime freelancers.

The Shifting Mix of Workers

She is adamant that not everyone is suited to freelancing.

"A lot of people go into freelancing saying they can write, and they think they're a freelancer," Shelley says. "And they're just not. They don't get it. They turn in sloppy work, they don't respond to emails, they turn in things late, they don't check sources, and they expect everything to be done for them, and don't treat you with respect.

"People who run their own businesses and are used to managing clients, they are the ones we love."

Thankfully help is at hand for those who want to get into freelancing. In July this year Melbourne-based entrepreneur

Bjarne Viken cofounded the website Digital Mined to teach freelancers how to build successful businesses.

He says many freelancers make simple mistakes such as failing to specifically respond to the client's requirements, responding with spelling and grammatical errors, and not articulating their areas of specialisation.

As a long time user of freelance services, he has witnessed a significant shift in the mix of workers in the marketplaces, and their expectations of income.

"A couple of years ago I struggled to get staff from the UK, Canada and the US at the rates that I was setting," Viken says. "But now if I put out a project I might get five or six candidates from those markets.

"We are going to see a shift where a lot of work that is priced at a higher level in Western countries going to go down in price quite simply because it can be outsourced."

11

Offices Will Become More Flexible Workplaces

Alison Maitland and Peter Thomson

Alison Maitland is a writer and speaker on work, gender, and leadership issues. Peter Thomson is director of Wisework Ltd. They coauthored Future Work: How Businesses Can Adapt and Thrive in the New World of Work.

While the rise of mobile working has placed the brick-and-mortar office under scrutiny, it will not disappear. Workers are social animals that thrive in the presence of each other; thoughtful discussions and bonds encourage productivity among colleagues and collaborators. However, with many employees unsatisfied with their work-life balance, the office of the future will be a meeting place rather than a workplace. Employees will be granted the flexibility to create their schedules, and the office itself will have spaces for them to work together or work independently, doing away with individual offices entirely. In this setting, leadership and management place more trust in workers, changing hierarchy and status within the company.

"The office should be a meeting place, not a working place. We can work anywhere, so it is social cohesion that becomes the important factor in physical premises."

> *Theo Rinsema, general manager,*
> *Microsoft Netherlands*

Alison Maitland and Peter Thomson, *Future Work: How Businesses Can Adapt and Thrive in the New World of Work*. New York: Palgrave Macmillan, 2011, pp. 79–84. Copyright © 2011 by Palgrave Macmillan. All rights reserved. Reproduced with permission.

Does the Office Have a Future?

The entrance to the Microsoft building in Amsterdam, a huge reflective-glass box next to Schiphol Airport, has the feel of an ultra-modern hotel lobby. People sit and stand around, chatting or waiting for appointments, bags and suitcases on the floor and laptops open on tables. Low sofas and coffee beckon from the hospitality corner.

There is no traditional reception desk with fixed phones. Black-suited receptionists emerge from behind a long white counter, greeting visitors, offering refreshments and using handheld messaging devices to alert hosts to their guests' arrival. Only the security barriers to the lifts and stairs signal that this is corporate territory.

The Netherlands office, designed for a world in which work is independent of time and location, is an experiment for Microsoft. Since it opened in 2008, it has attracted 500–1000 visitors a week, eager to glimpse the physical embodiment of 'anytime anywhere' work. Similar new Microsoft sites have followed in Belgium, France and Norway, and there has been interest from Argentina, Australia, India, Japan and Switzerland. The most common questions visitors ask are what it means for the individual, for productivity and for leadership.

> *The future is about 'empowering people to make decisions about how they want to work throughout a day.'*

Theo Rinsema, the Netherlands general manager, explains the concept behind the new design. With 'anytime anywhere' work, the role of the physical office changes, he says. Instead of being the location where employees gather at fixed times to do concentrated work, it becomes primarily a place for developing and maintaining connections between people.

On the first floor, color takes over from the black-and-white décor of the lobby. This is the 'community' floor, full of meeting spaces and people. The atmosphere is purposeful but informal. The busy restaurant has three-sided booths, with low-hanging lights over the tables. One long wall is covered with sound-absorbing, green fabric pieces held in place by what look like buttons.

At the far end of the floor is a series of meeting rooms with sofas, chairs and poufs but few tables, encouraging people to sink into whatever sitting, or even lying, position, they find most comfortable. There are tiny red chambers for private phone calls, and a wall of lockers with individuals' names chalked, kindergarten-style, on the doors.

Every employee has a badge with a chip inside which gives them access to the building and to all corporate information stored digitally, apart from personnel files. 'Connectedness' is emphasized by the open view from the first floor down into the lobby and up to the quieter second floor, which is dedicated to client meeting rooms. Here there are small workstations with sliding glass doors for concentrated, individual work, and open-plan desks that can be raised or lowered for preference.

Sevil Peach, the architect who led the design of the Microsoft building, says the future is about 'empowering people to make decisions about how they want to work throughout a day'.

The Brick-and-Mortar Office
Is Under Scrutiny

With the growth of mobile working around the world, the purpose of the bricks-and-mortar office is under scrutiny. There is pressure on organizations to reduce their carbon footprint, and potentially large scope to do so while making cost savings on office space if employees are spending more time working away from their desks.

Employees' expectations are adding to that pressure. According to an international survey commissioned by Cisco

Systems, the networking technology company, 60 percent of people believe they do not need to be in an office to be productive, a view that is strongest among employees in India, China and Brazil. Based on these findings, Cisco asks: 'Is the office really necessary?'

The answer is yes, but not in its conventional form. We do not expect, unlike some of the wilder predictions made back in the 1980s, that everyone will work from home and that offices will disappear any time soon. Even in the most technologically advanced companies like Microsoft, people are still social animals. Humans need to meet face-to-face, at least in early encounters, to develop fruitful relationships. Moreover, some people find solitary work difficult and stressful, while others thrive on it. What's important for most people is to have a healthy mix.

Offices will continue to be an important feature of the twenty-first century landscape. But the role of location in work is changing significantly.

'People like the choice of working at home but they often go spare if they are there for more than a couple of days a week,' says Alexi Marmot, professor of environment and facility management at University College London. 'There aren't many jobs that even the most thoughtful people can work at for weeks on end without the company of others. You somehow get empowered by the presence of other people. Evolutionary biologists and psychologists say that mankind is generally equipped to live in social groups.'

Online collaboration can be highly successful, but there are times when we have to be together in person to make things work. Advanced video-conferencing technology can simulate everyone being in the same room, even when they are dispersed around the globe, and it is becoming a good substitute for expensive and time-consuming business travel.

But it cannot entirely replace the energy that people derive from each other's physical presence, or the more personal, thoughtful discussions that bond colleagues and collaborators and make people feel valued.

Offices will continue to be an important feature of the twenty-first century landscape. But the role of location in work is changing significantly, and with it the role of management. . . .

From Workplace to Meeting Place

Employees of Microsoft in the Netherlands already had a lot of flexibility and were well-used to working from home at least part of the week, even before the move to the new building. But something was not right.

'They rated their work-life balance at 5.3 on a scale of 1 to 10 because they found it so difficult to stop working,' says Rinsema. 'So the question for us was: Have we adapted enough to this world of technology and globalization? Since we moved to the new building, the work-life balance score has gone up from 5.3 to 8.4, and is one of the highest in Microsoft worldwide.'

Productivity, measured by a model developed by Erasmus University in Rotterdam, has increased slightly following the move. The employee attrition rate is low at 8–9 percent a year, which is a mixed blessing: it demonstrates people's attachment to the new environment but it also holds back recruitment of new talent. The Dutch business wants to increase its female population, for example, from 17 percent to 25 percent by mid-2012.

The space per employee has fallen from 16 square meters to 11.5 square meters. Yet the occupancy rate has increased from just 25 percent in the previous offices to 40–45 percent, a big jump, though still below average office occupancy rates. 'We're a marketing and sales office so people should be outside,' explains Gonnie Been, manager of corporate communications and social innovation. 'But we also get our customers to visit us here.'

The 600 full-time employees, as well as the 300 contractors and interim staff, work from home one day a week on average, and the rest of the time at customers' sites or the Schiphol building. Even people who have to be present in the building to do their jobs, such as the receptionists and caterers, have a degree of autonomy, as they are able to arrange their own schedules.

Regarding the anywhere anytime workforce, you have to support and coach people that you do not expect them to be "always on."

A Focus on Changing Culture and Attitudes

Central to the success of the transfer has been the leadership team's focus on changing culture and attitudes. 'When we moved to this building, we moved from control to trust,' says Rinsema. 'We manage by output rather than presence. I don't know an organization that has put so much emphasis on changing leadership styles as we have. We separated status from hierarchy. There was some resistance during the journey.'

He agrees that future work is about empowering people, making them more productive and helping them with their work-life balance, or integration. 'It was perfectly clear to me that we had to further develop our leadership style in order to unleash employee empowerment. To be capable of leading based on trust, we as leaders realized that we had to look at our personal development, especially our personal drivers and control mechanisms.'

Rinsema has used a coach and facilitator to develop his team, including himself. At the start of the sessions, he asked what the program would be. The coach told him there was no program. This turned out to be the beginning of learning to let go.

'I gained a better insight into my personal control mechanisms and how much I depend on these,' he says. 'Fortunately I also gained insight into how I could loosen up a bit. I have the perception that I am much closer to the employees, with many more interactions through a variety of media. The balance between leading on the one hand and being a networked colleague on the other hand is, in this context, crucial. Regarding the anywhere anytime workforce, you have to support and coach people that you do not expect them to be "always on". You have to set the example as a leader.'

Many meetings are now virtual, and communication takes place via web technology such as the company's Live Meeting service, using webcams and headsets.

One highly symbolic change is that there are no individual offices. This is culturally very different from Microsoft's vast US headquarters in Redmond, Washington, where enclosed individual offices generally still matter and where the software giant has made huge investments in expanding its real estate portfolio on the campus and surrounding area in recent years.

'Nobody has a dedicated office, not even me,' says Rinsema. 'You find the ideal workspace depending on what you are doing.'

It is no accident that this pioneering building is in the Netherlands. It is easier to make the shift to future working styles in some cultural contexts than others. In general, northern Europe is more open to this than southern Europe, says Been. But there is resistance in America too. 'In the US, it still matters how long you have been in service, so cultural patterns are preventing it from changing,' she says. 'Europeans were more traditional and we're moving faster now. We must not become complacent. I'm working on how we get that constant change so that we stay ahead.'

One of the hardest things is breaking the link between status and position in the hierarchy. In the Netherlands, they are trying to do this by redefining status as the individual's contribution and leadership skills. People are encouraged both to move across functions and to develop individual expertise.

'Status comes through leadership, if people want to work with you,' says Been. 'The whole approach to the new world of work is that you need to be a personal leader—you need to lead your own life rather than being controlled by the boss as in the past—and if you're able to do that you are able to lead others. My next step could be towards more of a specialist role.'

Disconnecting Time from Work

One breakthrough followed an agreement that people were no longer expected to be in the office for meetings. 'The most difficult situation previously was when you had a few people who were physically there for the meeting and others who were dialing in, because those present assumed the others hadn't bothered to get there,' says Rinsema.

Many meetings are now virtual, and communication takes place via web technology such as the company's Live Meeting service, using webcams and headsets. There are no fixed telephone lines in the building, and this has cut costs, increased efficiency and changed the way people communicate.

'Sixty-eight per cent of phone calls used to end in voicemail,' he says. 'Now, we see if someone is available by starting a chat conversation through [Microsoft] Communicator, then we can move into a voice conversation if necessary and we can bring other people into the conversation and use web cams to replace physical meetings.'

Although employees already had flexibility, they felt uncomfortable about using the 'working day' to do something different like playing tennis, shopping or spending time with their children. The move to the new building has gone along with explicit permission to do these things.

'You disconnect time from work,' says Been. 'Work is a series of activities to get results. You can meet or communicate smarter. You can save at least 20 per cent of your time or energy to do other things. You finally do those things that you said: "If only I had time I would do that". There is no excuse any more.'

This does not mean that it is easy to change people's habitual ways of thinking and working. As Been points out, teleworking has been around as a concept since the 1980s, and the technology is available and advancing all the time. Yet people still spend hours sitting in traffic jams on the way to work in offices. Attitudes have to be constantly challenged. 'It's we people who keep the patterns going.'

12

Coworking: Is It Just a Fad or the Future of Business?

Adriana Lopez

Based in New Orleans, Adriana Lopez is an entrepreneur reporter at Forbes.com and contributor to Silicon Bayou News and NolaVie.

As contingent and nomadic workers shape the workforce, coworking is on the rise. In contrast to traditional office settings with workplace cubicles, coworking draws freelancers, contractors, and "solopreneurs"—working alone in home offices and coffee shops—to a single space, fostering collaboration and connections between like-minded professionals. Also, rather than competitiveness, coworking promotes networking and new business developments and opportunities; one study suggests that proximity is a factor in stimulating conversations, brainstorming, and problem solving. Finally, with feelings of isolation and disconnectedness facing many of today's professionals, those in coworking environments report boosts in productivity, confidence, and creativity.

Gone are the days of working in a traditional office setting, where cubicles separate colleagues and the only social interactions occur around the water cooler. The rise in coworking spaces around the world have left more people yearning for work environments that are collaborative, inspiring, and stimulating. And, nothing sounds more uninspiring than working in a 6x6 foot box and convening around a water dispenser, as if it were an oracle that could explain the meaning of life, or, at the very least, prophesize the outcome of *The Bachelor*.

Coworking has witnessed a significant resurgence over the past few years with the increase of the contingent workers—professionals who work independently as freelancers, contractors, or solopreneurs. The current state of the economy has shaped the workforce, as well as where and how we work.

Collaborative, Connected Environments

While people can no longer rely on their college degrees to manifest themselves into jobs, individuals have become more flexible and creative with their professions. They are starting businesses, creating jobs for themselves, and hustling for the next big opportunity. In fact, The Bureau of Labor Statistics estimates that by 2020, about 65 million Americans will be freelancers, temps, independent contractors and solopreneurs, making up about 40% of the workforce. Concurrently, workspaces are sprouting around the country in order to accommodate the growing number of nomadic workers.

These environments are not only stimulating, inspiring, and fun, but also lead to new business development and collaborations.

"As the American workforce trends toward independent contracting, freelance, and temping, co-working spaces and the collaborative, connective environments they create become more and more important—from both a social and professional standpoint," said Beau Button, Founder of WebDevrs and the Dojo in New Orleans. "No longer the exception, coworking spaces will be the rule."

The Dojo is a digitally focused workspace in New Orleans anchored by mobile and web app development firm Web-

Devrs. Their mission is to create a place where developers, designers, programmers, and the creative alike can come together to harness their creative energy.

"Co-working spaces are melting pots of creativity," added Button. "They generate a level of synergy that results from the proximity and collaboration of like-minded people. New relationships are developed. Ideas are challenged. Problems are solved."

Today, coworking comes with benefits beyond just WiFi and unlimited coffee. Professional, personal, and social gains come as added bonuses that are more advantageous than working in a coffee shop or home office/living room/dining room. These environments are not only stimulating, inspiring, and fun, but also lead to new business development and collaborations, as well as increased levels of productivity and income as a result of being part of an expanding business network.

Proximity a Stimulating Factor

Proximity seems to be a factor in stimulating collaborations and innovation in the work environment. According to a study that was recently conducted by a team at Harvard University, it has been concluded that geographic proximity is valuable in collaboration, despite living in an era dominated by the Internet, wireless communication, and e-mail. Findings in 35,000 academic papers showed that physical proximity mattered after concluding that correlations between the most cited papers and the close distances between authors led to more impactful publications. Although the study focused on innovation in science, the data proved that face-to-face communication was more impactful, leading to less agenda-driven and more fluid conversations, brainstorming, problem solving, and serendipitous accidents.

"Despite working in similar fields, people are not competitive in coworking environments," explained Andrea Chen, executive director of Propeller Incubator. "Everyone finds their own niche and often encourage peer-to-peer learning and collaboration."

Chen's incubator is the only socially minded incubator in New Orleans, and one of the few that exists nationwide. After opening the 10,000 square foot space in January [2014], Propeller is almost at capacity with tenants that range from social entrepreneurs, professional service providers, and fellows from their accelerator program.

Chen also added that the collaborative environment has already fostered business partnerships and business development, as desk neighbors often become each others' clients or business partners. In an example, two of the Propeller tenants, RapJab and FitLot, developed an app together called NOLAparks.com for the Super Bowl's CodeMakrs Super Challenge, and won the competition's innovation award. The app is currently being used internally by the City of New Orleans.

People who work in coworking spaces reported to be more productive, confident, and creative.

"People no longer want walls around them," said Chen. "They want to make connections and feel connected in a day and age that is so tech minded and often disconnected."

More Productive, Confident, and Creative

Isolation and feeling disconnected is a challenge that many of today's professionals feel, whether it's from the cubicle's cork panel wall, late night coding at home, or a long day of becoming one with your laptop at the local coffee shop. In addition to the advent of social media sites like Twitter and Facebook, today's generation is constantly finding ways to connect, and yearn to find that kind of activity daily.

In an annual survey conducted by Deskmag, people who work in coworking spaces reported to be more productive, confident, and creative. Reports showed that 71% of people surveyed were more creative, 62% reported that their measure of work improved significantly, and 90% said they felt more confident when coworking. Additionally, 70% reported that they felt healthier than they did working in a traditional office setting. The statistics are the result of being part of a supportive and expanding network that offers flexibility in when you choose to work and whom you choose to work with. Aspects such as reduced stress also become a factor, as most people were able to minimize their commute time and were less likely to become victims of office politics.

It's not just those who are self-employed that are benefiting. As coworking becomes the future of business, larger companies like AT&T and Zappos are starting to capitalize on this new shift, confirming that the benefits are real. And, while the workforce continues to shift, traditional office settings will become as obsolete as fax machines and dial up Internet.

Organizations to Contact

The editors have compiled the following list of organizations concerned with the issues debated in this book. The descriptions are derived from materials provided by the organizations. All have publications or information available for interested readers. The list was compiled on the date of publication of the present volume; names, addresses, phone and fax numbers, and e-mail and Internet addresses may change. Be aware that many organizations take several weeks or longer to respond to inquiries, so allow as much time as possible.

American Farm Bureau Federation (AFBF)
600 Maryland Ave. SW, Suite 1000W, Washington, DC 20024
(202) 406-3600
website: www.fb.org

The American Farm Bureau Federation (AFBF) is an independent, nongovernmental, voluntary organization governed by and representing farm and ranch families united for the purpose of analyzing agricultural problems and formulating action to achieve educational improvement, economic opportunity, and social advancement, and thereby promote the national well-being. The AFBF website offers a newsroom, video, and information on farming issues, legislation, and legal advocacy.

American Society of Mechanical Engineers (ASME)
2 Park Ave., New York, NY 10016-5990
(800) 843-2763
website: www.asme.org

Founded in 1880, the American Society of Mechanical Engineers (ASME) is a 120,000-member professional organization focused on technical, educational, and research issues of the engineering and technology community. ASME conducts one of the world's largest technical publishing operations, holds numerous technical conferences worldwide, and offers hundreds of professional development courses each year. It publishes the magazine *Mechanical Engineering.*

The GEMS Clubs: Girls Excelling at Math and Science
e-mail: info@gemsclub.org
website: www.gemsclub.org

The GEMS Clubs: Girls Excelling at Math and Science have been working since 1994 to increase interest in science, technology, engineering, and mathematics (STEM) for girls in elementary and middle school and to expose girls to the fun and wonder of these fields. The organization has helped launch clubs worldwide. Online, it offers information and links for girls and educators as well as sections dedicated to STEM learning.

IEEE Robotics and Automation Society (IEEE-RAS)
445 Hoes Lane, Piscataway Township, NJ   08854
e-mail: ras@ieee.org
website: www.ieee-ras.org

Part of the Institute of Electrical and Electronics Engineers (IEEE), IEEE Robotics and Automation Society (IEEE-RAS) is interested in both applied and theoretical issues in robotics and automation. Robotics is defined to include intelligent machines and systems used, for example, in space exploration, human services, or manufacturing; whereas automation includes the use of automated methods in various applications, for example, factory, office, home, laboratory automation, or transportation systems to improve performance and productivity. The organization publishes *Robotics & Automation Magazine.*

Institute of Electrical and Electronics Engineers (IEEE)
445 Hoes Lane, Piscataway Township, NJ   08854
website: www.ieee.org

The core purpose of the Institute of Electrical and Electronics Engineers (IEEE) is to foster technological innovation and excellence for the benefit of humanity. It aims to be essential to the global technical community and to technical professionals everywhere, and be universally recognized for the contributions of technology and of technical professionals in improving global conditions. IEEE publishes a monthly magazine, *IEEE Spectrum*.

Institute for the Future (IFTF)
201 Hamilton Ave., Palo Alto, CA 94301
(650) 854-6322
e-mail: info@iftf.org
website: www.iftf.org

Institute for the Future (IFTF) is an independent nonprofit research group that specializes in technological, business, and social trends. Based in northern California's Silicon Valley, it was founded in 1968 by a group of former RAND Corporation researchers with a grant from the Ford Foundation. The IFTF website features sections such as Foresight Tools and History of the Future. Among its programs are Future of Work, Future of Learning, and Ten-Year Forecast.

Robotic Industries Association (RIA)
900 Victors Way, Suite 140, Ann Arbor, MI 48106
(734) 994-6088 • fax: (734) 994-3338
website: www.robotics.org

Founded in 1974, the Robotic Industries Association (RIA) is North America's only trade association focused exclusively on robotics. More than 250 of its member companies represent leading robot manufacturers, system integrators, end users, and researchers. RIA also provides robotics news and information on its website, Robotics Online, and publishes an e-newsletter.

US Department of Labor (DOL)
Frances Perkins Building, 200 Constitution Ave. NW
Washington, DC 20210
(866) 487-2365
website: www.dol.gov

The mission of the US Department of Labor (DOL) is to foster, promote, and develop the welfare of the wage earners, job seekers, and retirees of the United States; improve working conditions; advance opportunities for profitable employment; and assure work-related benefits and rights. Online, DOL provides information and statistics on job growth, employment, and wages as well as several occupation publications, including *Beyond the Numbers* and *Monthly Labor Review.*

Bibliography

Books

Erik Brynjolfsson and Andrew McAfee

The Second Machine Age: Work, Progress, and Prosperity in a Time of Brilliant Technologies. New York: W.W. Norton, 2014.

Paul K. Conkin

A Revolution Down on the Farm: The Transformation of American Agriculture Since 1929. Lexington: University Press of Kentucky, 2009.

Tyler Cowen

Average Is Over: Powering America Beyond the Age of the Great Stagnation. New York: Dutton, 2013.

Martin Ford

The Lights in the Tunnel: Automation, Accelerating Technology, and the Economy of the Future. North Charleston, SC: CreateSpace, 2009.

Edward E. Gordon

Future Jobs: Solving the Employment and Skills Crisis. Santa Barbara, CA: Praeger, 2013.

Michio Kaku

Physics of the Future: How Science Will Shape Human Destiny and Our Daily Lives by the Year 2100. New York: Doubleday, 2011.

Alison Maitland and Peter Thomson

Future Work: Changing Organizational Culture for the New World of Work, 2nd ed. New York: Palgrave Macmillan, 2014.

Viktor Mayer-Schönberger and Kenneth Cukier	*Big Data: A Revolution That Will Transform How We Live, Work, and Think*. Boston: Houghton Mifflin Harcourt, 2013.
Federico Pistono	*Robots Will Steal Your Job, but That's OK: How to Survive the Economic Collapse and Be Happy*. North Charleston, SC: CreateSpace, 2012.
Eric Schmidt and Jared Cohen	*The New Digital Age: Reshaping the Future of People, Nations, and Business*. New York: Alfred A. Knopf, 2013.

Periodicals and Internet Sources

Thomas H. Davenport	"It's Already Time to Kill the 'Data Scientist' Title," *CIO Journal*, April 30, 2014.
Thomas H. Davenport and D.J. Patil	"Data Scientist: The Sexiest Job of the 21st Century," *Harvard Business Review*, October 2012.
Christopher Doering	"Want a Job? Agriculture Industry Teeming with Them," *USA Today*, July 14, 2013.
Shannon Douglass	"Commentary: Future Prospects Remain Bright for Agricultural Graduates," *Ag Alert*, February 15, 2012. http://agalert.com.
Economist	"The Onrushing Wave," January 18, 2014.
Aaron Gordon	"You, Yes You, Can Analyze Data, Too," *Pacific Standard*, April 21, 2014.

Freeman A. Hrabowski III	"The Future of Women in Tech," *Baltimore Sun*, February 16, 2014.
Knowledge @Wharton	"A Smaller Slice of the Pie: Why Technology Is No Longer Creating Jobs," March 13, 2013. http:// knowledge.wharton.upenn.edu.
John Mercier	"The Jobs of the Future in National Security and Intelligence," *National Defense*, July 2011.
Jonathan O'Connell	"In Offices of the Future, Receptionists Are Virtual, Walls Are for Writing On and Flexibility Trumps All," *Washington Post*, March 14, 2014.
Catherine Rampell	"It Takes a B.A. to Find a Job as a File Clerk," *New York Times*, February 19, 2013.
Robert Samuelson	"Technology a Barrier to Job Creation?," *Real Clear Markets*, July 15, 2013. www.realclearmarkets.com.
John Shinal	"Future Economy: Many Will Lose Their Jobs to Computers," *USA Today*, March 21, 2014.
Claire Shipman and Katty Kay	"Women Will Rule Business," *Time*, May 14, 2009.
Derek Thompson	"What Jobs Will the Robots Take?," *Atlantic*, January 13, 2014.

Index

G

H

I

J

K

L